NEW MERMAIDS

NEW MERMAIDS

General editor: Brian Gibbons
Professor of English Literature, University of Münster

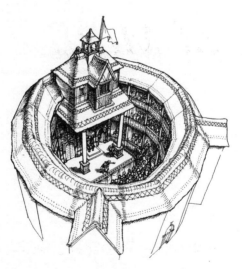

Reconstruction of an Elizabethan theatre
by C. Walter Hodges

NEW MERMAIDS

John Webster

The Duchess of Malfi

4th edition

edited by Brian Gibbons

**Professor of English Literature
University of Münster**

A & C Black • London
WW Norton • New York

Fourth edition 2001
A & C Black (Publishers) Limited
35 Bedford Row
London WC1R 4JH
ISBN 0-7136-5061-3

© 2001 A & C Black (Publishers) Limited

First New Mermaid edition 1964
Second edition 1983
Ernest Benn Limited

Third edition 1993
A & C Black (Publishers) Limited

Published in the United States of America
by W. W. Norton & Company Inc.
500 Fifth Avenue, New York, NY 10110
ISBN 0-393-90091-6

CIP catalogue records for this book are available
from the British Library and the Library of
Congress.

Printed in Great Britain by
The Guernsey Press Co., Ltd, Guernsey, Channel
Islands

CONTENTS

ACKNOWLEDGEMENTS

In preparing this new edition I have, like all editors, incurred debts to predecessors, especially F. L. Lucas, John Russell Brown, Elizabeth Brennan, and David Carnegie, D. C. Gunby and Antony Hammond. I have attempted to acknowledge debts to other scholars and critics in footnotes and the list of Further Reading. In preparing the edition it has been a pleasure to work with such consistently able, good-humoured and level-headed colleagues at Münster and Bedford Row – Angela Stock, Christian Krug, Anne-Julia Zwierlein, Lydia Remke, Anne Watts, Tesni Hollands and Katie Taylor.

New Edition 2001   BRIAN GIBBONS

INTRODUCTION

The Author

John Webster was born in 1578 or 1579. He was the eldest son of a maker of coaches and wagons. The family home and business was in Cow Lane, Smithfield, a noisy, smelly, crowded district of London which included the cattle market and Newgate prison. During this period the coachbuilding trade boomed: the family business continued to make utilitarian carts but expanded to satisfy the new demand for fashionable coaches; it also hired out transport, and may have provided transport for funerals and city pageants. With prosperity came respectability. Webster's father styled himself 'gentleman' and became a member of the Company of Merchant Taylors, and Webster very probably, therefore, went to the Merchant Taylors' School (though there is no documentary evidence). His younger brother Edward earned the honour of becoming a member of the Merchant Taylors by working in the family business, whereas the playwright himself did not join at the normal age but in his late thirties, in 1615, using his father's connections to buy his membership. This was about the time that his father died.

Edward took on the expanding business. It is possible that John may have continued to be involved in the family firm, at any rate his background in trade was not something that he was allowed to forget – in 1617 he was mocked as 'Crabbed Websterio, / The playwright, cart-wright'.[1] Whatever his motives for becoming a member of the company of Merchant Taylors, it did lead to a literary commission, to write the Lord Mayor's pageant in 1624. As late as 1632 a satirist connects Webster to his family roots, holding that Webster's brother refused to lend a coach for a funeral because he 'swore thay all weare hired to conuey / the Malfi Dutches sadly on her way'.[2]

After leaving school Webster probably entered the New Inn and then Middle Temple (one of the Inns of Court) in 1598. At that time, attending the Inns of Court did not necessarily mean that one had a legal career in mind – a young gentleman might acquire a

---

[1] Henry Fitzgeffrey, *Notes from Black-Fryers*, 1617.

[2] cit. Forker p. 58. I am indebted to Forker's admirably scrupulous and clear account of Webster's life, drawing on the best scholarship: he shows how little hard evidence there is for Webster's education and earlier years, and treats speculations with due caution.

more general education and 'finish' there (Marston, Overbury and
Ford, writers whom Webster knew, had been students at the Middle
Temple). Throughout Webster's career an interest in the law continued to be important, and this is circumstantial evidence for his
having been a student there; but his future was to be in another
booming London business – the theatre.

In the records for 1602–3 of Henslowe, the theatre manager/
entrepreneur, Webster's name appears as one of the hack playwrights writing in collaboration. The records are incomplete and
two of the plays referred to are lost, but they were probably written
fast to satisfy a strong demand for new material. They are *Caesar's
Fall* (lost) by Munday, Drayton, Webster, Middleton, Dekker;
Christmas Comes but Once a Year (lost) by Heywood, Webster,
Chettle, Dekker; and *Lady Jane* (probably the basis for a play which
does survive and was published in 1607 as *Sir Thomas Wyatt*) by
Chettle, Dekker, Webster, Heywood, Smith. These plays were for
companies of adult actors at amphitheatre playhouses. In 1604
Webster wrote significant additions to John Marston's play *The
Malcontent* (originally written for the boys' company of
Blackfriars) when it was acquired by Shakespeare's company, the
King's Men, to be acted at the Globe. In the same year Webster col-
laborated with Dekker on a play, *Westward Ho*, for the fashionable
and more expensive boys' company at Paul's, an indoor theatre.
This was successful enough to provoke Jonson, Chapman and
Marston to write in response *Eastward Ho* (1605) for Blackfriars,
and for Dekker and Webster to write a follow up, *Northward Ho*,
for Paul's. Their two plays were published in 1607.

Webster married in 1606, and his first child was born two
months after the wedding – a fact which might be interesting in
relation to the Duchess' difficulties in keeping her pregnancy secret.
But there is a gap, and no new writing is known of between 1605
and 1612, when the most important period of his work as a playwright begins with the performance of *The White Devil* by Queen
Anne's Men at the Red Bull in 1612. Its first reception was disap-
pointing; nevertheless he was working on a new play, *The Duchess
of Malfi*, in 1612, when Prince Henry died, and Webster broke off
to write the non-dramatic elegy *A Monumental Column*, dedicated
to the King's favourite, Robert Carr.

The Duchess of Malfi must have been first performed before the
end of 1614 because the actor William Ostler, who played Antonio,
died on 16 December 1614. The play was an immediate success,
and has continued to be so to the present day. In 1615 Webster
wrote additions to the sixth edition of Overbury's prose *Characters*.
There is speculation that there may be a lost play, *Guise*, in the
years before the last of Webster's major works, the play *The Devil's
Law Case*, 1617–18.

The Duchess of Malfi and *The Devil's Law Case* were published in 1623. Thereafter Webster continued to write plays, but only in collaboration: *Anything for a Quiet Life* with Middleton in 1621, and then a series of plays with old colleagues: in 1624, *A Late Murder of the Son upon the Mother, or, Keep the Widow Waking*, with Dekker, Ford and Rowley; in c. 1624–5, *A Cure for a Cuckold*, with Rowley. In c. 1625–6 Webster with Ford and Massinger completed *The Fair Maid of the Inn*, begun by Fletcher; in c. 1626–7 he wrote *Appius and Virginia*, probably with Heywood, although Webster's name appears alone on the title page. Webster had a success with the strikingly lavish and extravagant pageant he undertook for the Merchant Taylors in 1624, *Monuments of Honour*, celebrating the election of their member, John Gore, as Lord Mayor. Exactly where and when Webster died is not known, but it was probably in the 1630s.

The Play

From Page to Stage

The Duchess and Antonio were in fact real historical figures. She was born Giovanna d'Aragona about 1478, married aged twelve to Alfonso Piccolomini, Duke of Malfi from 1493 until his death in 1498. Widowed, she was left with a daughter and a son, and ruled Malfi as regent with some success. She had a sister and two brothers; the eldest, Lodovico, had a promising career as a soldier before entering the Church and becoming a cardinal in 1494. This did not prevent him fighting in two campaigns. He continued to be a cardinal and died peacefully at Rome.

Antonio Bologna was brought up at Naples in the royal court, served Federico the last Aragonian King of Naples and followed him into exile. Returning on Federico's death, Antonio accepted the post of major-domo in the household of the Duchess. In 1510 he left her service and went to Ancona. That November the Duchess, supposedly on a pilgrimage to Loretto, joined him, they being secretly married and with two children. A third was born in Ancona where they lived openly as man and wife. Her brother Lodovico caused trouble for them with the authorities and they moved to Siena, but they had to move again, and en route to Venice were intercepted; Antonio and his eldest son escaped and reached Milan but the Duchess, the other children and her waiting woman were arrested, taken to a castle under armed guard, and never seen again. In October 1513 Antonio was stabbed to death in the street. Alfonso, the Duchess' son by her first marriage, ruled as Duke of Malfi until he died in 1559.

The story of the Duchess of Malfi and Antonio is in the twenty-sixth novella in Part One of the Italian Bandello's *Novelle* (4 vol-

umes, 1554–73). An adaptation of Bandello in French was written
by François de Belleforest as *Histoires Tragiques* (1565). An English
version, faithful to Belleforest, was made by William Painter, *The
second tome of the palace of pleasure* (1567). This is Webster's
principal source for *The Duchess of Malfi*.

Bandello probably knew the real-life Antonio personally – and
the outline of events up to the arrest of the Duchess in Bandello is
as in Webster. Then, Bandello relates, the Duchess was escorted to
one of the castles in her Duchy where she and her children and waiting woman were later strangled (no word of torture); meanwhile
Antonio in Milan was unsuccessfully trying to find a protector, failing to prevent his property in Naples from being confiscated, and
still hoping for a reconciliation with the brothers of the Duchess.
The brothers hired an assassin, but this man, a Neapolitan, warned
Antonio; the brothers then hired a second hit-man, Daniele da
Bozolo, a Lombard captain, who with three accomplices killed
Antonio and got clean away.

Belleforest's version is four times longer, adds dialogues and solil-
oquies, considerably – but with little art – develops the characters,
and with heavy moralism alters the point of view: he strongly dis-
approves of the secret marriage between a person of royal blood
and a commoner, and censures its folly and wantonness. Antonio is
more prudential, ambitious and sentimental in motive than he is in
Bandello.[3] At the same time Belleforest's Duchess, like his Antonio,
arouses pathos: she is permitted to explain her own actions passionately and cogently at the point of death, and she and Antonio are
recognised as also possessing charm and merit. Belleforest calls the
story a tragedy and firmly divides the narrative into three Acts, the
first ending with the marriage, the second with Antonio's flight to
Ancona, the last with Antonio's death. These features are important
to Webster.

Painter in his English version makes no significant alterations to
Belleforest, so that Webster's principal source presents a moralising
and censorious account of the widow:

---

[3] Webster had read about lycanthropia in Edward Grimestone's translation of Simon
Goulart, *Admirable and Memorable Histories* (1607), so he might have read in the
same volume an account of the Duchess of Malfi's romance with Antonio which
Goulart condemns as unchaste. No less strong is the condemnation by Thomas
Beard, *Theatre of God's Judgements* (1597), who presented the story in terms of
'whoredomes committed vnder Colour of Marriage'. On the other hand George
Whetstone, *Heptameron of Civil Discourses* (1582), writes that though the
Duchess made a 'base choice' nevertheless 'a woman looseth none of her general
titles of dignitie by matching w' her inferior'. See also Boklund p. 19.

> This Lady waxed very weary of lying alone, and grieved her heart to
> be without a match, specially in the night, when the secret silence and
> darkness of the same presented before the eyes of her mind, the image
> of the pleasure which she felt in the life time of her deceased lord and
> husband ... 'Alas (said she) ... But what desire is this? I have a cer-
> tain unacquainted lust'.

The Duchess disdains the 'light' young gentlemen cavorting on their
fine horses in the city of Naples, and Painter grants that although
she is in thrall to her sexual appetite when she does fall in love, her
choice Antonio is 'one of the wisest and most perfect gentlemen that
the land of Naples that time brought forth, and for his beauty, proportion, galantness, valiance, and good grace, without comparison',
and Painter adds 'Who then could blame this fair Princess'. While
showing some tenderness in depicting the inner emotional life of the
main characters, and granting the Duchess passion, dignity and
pathos when describing her strangling, Painter maintains the moralising frame imposed by Belleforest: to give way to sexual passion,
to make a socially unequal marriage, to neglect one's duty, is to
deserve such punishment.

In designing the play Webster makes substantial changes and
introduces new material. He gives as much importance to
Ferdinand as to the Cardinal, so that the action centres on the con-
flict between the two brothers and the Duchess and Antonio.
Webster invents a wholly new character, Julia, to reflect aspects of
the Duchess and illuminate the character of her brother the
Cardinal. He invents the visit to Malfi in Act I by the Cardinal and
Ferdinand, and their hiring of Bosola then, and he combines the
wooing and the wedding, making Cariola witness to both (in
Painter the marriage does not take place until the next day).
Webster brings forward the discovery of the Duchess' secret (in
Painter it is placed after the birth of her second child) and he invents
the clue, the dropped horoscope, as well as having Bosola detect it.
Ferdinand's entire visit to Malfi in Act III and the crucial scene in
the Duchess' chamber, III.ii, are wholly Webster's invention.
Webster follows Painter in the movements leading to the Duchess'
arrest, but he then invents the sequence in which Bosola devises torments for the Duchess and the episode when Ferdinand gives her the
severed hand. In Act V Webster invents much of the action, the
entire Echo scene, the Julia scene, the accidental manner of
Antonio's death, the episode in which the Cardinal is trapped, and
the final deaths of the brothers and of Bosola himself – in Painter
the brothers live on and Bozola escapes after his efficient contract-
killing of Antonio. Webster transforms Bosola into a major character who is present from the beginning – in doing so he combines
several minor figures in Painter, whose Bozola is only a minor role
at the very end. Bosola's ancestry is chiefly in other plays –

Flamineo in Webster's own tragedy *The White Devil*, Vindice in *The Revenger's Tragedy*, Malevole in *The Malcontent*, and even something of Hamlet himself.

Webster's portrayal of the brothers gives them exaggerated personalities: by contrast his Duchess is emotionally more direct and emphasises the affection and companionship in her marriage to a social inferior. Painter, following Belleforest, condemns the Duchess as a wanton widow,[4] but <u>Webster seems deliberately to present a more complex and sympathetic view of his characters</u> and of the significance of the story.[5] He was very aware of the divergent attitudes associated with different Jacobean audiences, and his largely sympathetic attitude to the Duchess' choice of love is in tune with the taste catered for by the King's Men for whom he wrote the play.[6] The relationship between dramatic fiction and historical fact is not straightforward or direct. One should guard against a cut-and-dried, simplistic view of cultural attitudes, which might vary according to education, class, or age (the younger generation perhaps readier to question convention). In addition a spectator's attitude might temporarily soften under the sway of a powerful play, entertaining ideas and feelings that would not survive the cold of everyday real life.

One indication that Webster is conscious of writing for a par-

---

[4] Some critics have interpreted the play as if it presented the point of view of Painter; among these Joyce E. Peterson (1978) is an extreme, claiming that the Duchess abandons her duty to indulge private desire. William Empson allowed himself to be provoked into taking an opposite view: 'the moral of this play, driven home as with the sledgehammer of Dickens I should have thought, is not that the Duchess was wanton but that her brothers were sinfully proud' – William Empson, 'Mine Eyes Dazzle', *E in C*, vol. 14 (1964).

[5] Andrew Gurr, *Playgoing*, p. 149, has described as a significant 'new' line Shakespeare's celebration in the 1590s of the power of love over parental authority in *Romeo and Juliet* and the comedies. Gurr notes that the rival Henslowe companies, whose playhouses were north of the river Thames, made no attempt to copy this newly popular taste, indeed after 1600 'they actively opposed it and the challenge to citizen views about marriage which it embodied'. In *Romeo and Juliet* Shakespeare evidently relied on, as well as augmented, audience sympathy for his young lovers when they disobey their parents and marry in secret, although Shakespeare's source for *Romeo and Juliet*, Brooke, was firmly disapproving.

[6] There are significant real-life instances in England at this time of noble widows remarrying; nor in England were attitudes to clandestine marriages invariably condemnatory. As to English noble persons marrying their inferiors, one famous and popular case was the Duchess of Suffolk, who in 1552 married her servant. For instances see Brennan, pp. 134–5, Forker, pp. 299–300.

ticular audience is his quoting so often in *The Duchess of Malfi* from Sidney's *Arcadia*, for this was the favourite reading of young gallants and university men, and, as Andrew Gurr notes, the 'fashion generated by Shakespeare's last plays has closest affinities to Sidney's *Arcadia*, and that affinity, together with the availability of the plays at Blackfriars, most convenient to the Inns of Court, helped confirm the King's Men in their grip on the upper sections of the playgoing market'.[7] Webster knew he was facing the most educated audience, the top of the market, and *The Duchess of Malfi* is tailor-made to suit that discriminating, fashionable taste. The dialogue has a complex texture: Webster read widely and often incorporated directly what he read, from single finely phrased and exotic metaphors such as 'we are the stars' tennis-balls' to a description of a bizarre mental illness called lycan-thropia. The many detailed verbal borrowings, parallels, and quotations have been discussed in the pioneering 1927 edition by Lucas, also in R. W. Dent's study *John Webster's Borrowing* (1960), and Gunnar Boklund's *'The Duchess of Malfi': Sources, Themes, Characters* (1962). Webster also translated the verbal to the visual: thus a long narrative episode in Sidney's *Arcadia*, Cecopria's psychological torture of the princesses, gave him the idea of the silent display of waxwork bodies in IV.ii of *The Duchess of Malfi*.[8]

Non-verbal Dimensions

The relatively small competitive world of Jacobean theatre encour-aged in the playwrights a good deal of borrowing from, parody of, and allusion to, one another's works not only in verbal terms but also non-verbal and visual codes.[9] Writing *The Duchess of Malfi* for Shakespeare's company the King's Men, Webster borrows distinct

---

[7] Gurr, *Playgoing*, p. 168. Earlier, pp. 100–2, Gurr describes the way one very learned spectator, William Drummond of Hawthornden, read and annotated another text used by Webster: Alexander's *Four Monarchicke Tragedies*. Webster borrowed intensively from a wide and eclectic range of texts when writing *The Duchess of Malfi*, and only a selective sample can be indicated in the footnotes to the play. For a fuller account see the major studies by Dent and Boklund.

[8] It is also true that Webster may have been influenced by the life-size wax effigy of Prince Henry, richly clothed, which lay on top of the coffin and was borne through the London streets in the funeral procession in 1612: see David Bergeron, 'The wax figures in *The Duchess of Malfi*', *SEL* 18 (1978), pp. 331–9. Webster broke off composition of Act III of *The Duchess of Malfi* to write an elegy on the occasion.

[9] See e.g. notes to the present edition at I.i.321 and I.i.350, IV.ii.1 and IV.ii.108, IV.ii.278–95 and IV.ii.331, V.iii.0, V.v.46.

non-verbal, visual images from several Shakespeare plays.[10] Webster's business with keys, darkness, prison-cells, spying and religious robes visually recalls *Measure for Measure* (1604), while concentration on the silent and inert human body, whether unconscious or dead or made of stone, is a visual feature of other recent King's Men plays, *The Winter's Tale* (1610–11) and *Cymbeline* (1609–10), and of the earlier Jacobean plays, *Othello* (1604), *King Lear* (1605), *The Revenger's Tragedy* (1605); but among sources of Webster's visual borrowings, *Othello* stands out as an exemplary case, and to pause on it for a moment may bring out some general principles of Webster's dramaturgy.

The very actor who had created the role of Othello, Richard Burbage, was to play Webster's Ferdinand, and Webster must have hoped not only that parallels to *Othello* in *The Duchess of Malfi* would be recognised but that the calculated difference in inflection would be recognised too, at least by a proportion of the spectators – that section which, as Jacobean dramatists liked to emphasise, had more understanding. In *Othello* Desdemona drops a handkerchief (with an embroidered pattern of strawberries on it) which Iago acquires; he uses it to incriminate her fatally in the eyes of Othello, her murderously jealous husband. Webster makes a variation on this: in *The Duchess of Malfi* Antonio, while taking out a handkerchief to stanch a nosebleed, drops a piece of paper on which is written his new-born son's horoscope, and it is this which Bosola finds: he then uses it to incriminate the Duchess in the eyes of her murderously jealous brothers. This whole episode is not in Painter, Webster evidently was struck by seeing how in Shakespeare's play the first, deadly clue is a piece of white material, a real object which the spectators can see the actors carry about. He makes sure that the visual parallel is retained, while he transfers importance from a handkerchief to a paper.[11]

---

[10] When Ferdinand produces a severed hand Webster may intend an allusion to Shakespeare's *Titus Andronicus*, first performed some twenty years earlier. Alternatively, or in addition, Webster may have got the idea from Bandello, in the novella immediately preceding the story of *The Duchess of Malfi* or from Barnaby Riche, *The Famous History of Herodotus* (1584), but since in Webster's day *Titus Andronicus* was so famous – as Ben Jonson in 1614 wryly concedes in the Induction to *Bartholmew Fair* – and since nobody who has seen *Titus Andronicus* can ever forget the effect of the severed hand, if Webster did read the Bandello novella or Riche he would have been reminded of Shakespeare and have seen the tremendous theatrical potential of the idea. Webster is in turn paid homage as a deviser of horror by his fellow playwright Thomas Middleton in *The Changeling*, where the malcontent De Flores produces a severed finger which he presents to the appalled heroine.

[11] There is an ominous dropped letter in *The Spanish Tragedy* to which Webster may also slyly allude.

In III.ii of *The Duchess of Malfi* Webster borrows largely from IV.iii of *Othello*. The Duchess, like Desdemona, is seen making preparations for bed: Desdemona removes jewels – 'Lay by these': Webster's Duchess too removes jewels and unpins her hair;[12] but whereas Desdemona is in troubled mood (Othello having ordered her to bed after abusing her in public as 'that cunning whore of Venice'), Webster's Duchess is happily conversing with her maid Cariola and her husband Antonio (although the audience know that Ferdinand has secretly acquired the key to her chamber and intends to use it 'this night'). Ferdinand's surprise entry with the dagger to 'force confession from her' corresponds to Othello's entry (at V.ii) to force a confession from Desdemona before stifling her – but notice that Othello explicitly decides *against* a dagger:[13]

> Yet I'll not shed her blood
> Nor scar that whiter skin of hers than snow
> And smooth as monumental alabaster   (*Othello*, V.ii.3–5)

Webster's most emphatic borrowing from *Othello* is an Act later, in IV.ii, where he presents the strangling of the Duchess and her revival, like Desdemona, to die finally with words of love and piety on her lips. But to place the death of the central character before the final Act, as Webster does, finds no parallel in *Othello*; instead, it is in Shakespeare's *Antony and Cleopatra* (1606–7). There the hero Antony dies after botching his suicide (by the sword) in Act IV, leaving Act V to confused intrigue from which Cleopatra finally frees herself by suicide. In Webster it is the heroine not the hero who dies in Act IV, but Webster's heroine does die like Shakespeare's with dignity and his Antonio too does suffer a botched death by the sword – though neither are suicides.

Tragical-Satirical

Webster is nowhere more characteristically Jacobean than in his conceiving the play as a tragic hybrid, including elements generic to the currently fashionable Jacobean revenge play – the court setting, spying, melancholy, madness, multiple murders. This is itself a powerful formula, but Webster combines with it features of high tragedy – the distinct tragic career of an exceptional but flawed

---

[12] Desdemona first tells her maid Emilia to give her 'my nightly wearing', then tells her 'unpin me here', referring either to her gown or her hair. Desdemona later declares she would not commit adultery 'by this heavenly light' and Emilia retorts that she would not either – but she might well do it 'i'th'dark' if the price was right – just the joke to catch Webster's eye.

[13] Notice too that it is to a statue of herself *in alabaster* that Webster's Duchess contrasts herself.

figure, brought to ruin by a concatenation of circumstances which take the shape of ironic fate. A defining characteristic of *The Duchess of Malfi* is the degree to which scepticism is incorporated in its design, and here Webster's model is predominantly Shakespeare. It is Hamlet who memorably remarks that a black suit of clothes, sighs and tears and dejected expression, are merely a code, a sign-system, not to be trusted:

> These indeed seem,
> For they are actions that a man might play   (*Hamlet*, I.ii.83–4)

Webster's *The Duchess of Malfi* is a tragedy as Painter's story is not; but it is a tragedy qualified above all by Shakespearean innovations to that mode: it gains much from the destabilising energies of scepticism as they engage sharply with a fundamentally religious conception of human life.[14] The play quotes (as does Shakespeare) from the sceptical Montaigne, though it is also in touch with stoicism – it is written in a cultural moment much concerned with guilt and damnation, and satire is an important informing element in its writing. It is a hybrid through and through. Some modern scholars interpret it as showing a Calvinistic bias, whereas others consider it even consistent with Jacobean Anglicanism. *The Duchess of Malfi* struck a contemporary Italian spectator as an attack on Catholicism and the Church of Rome – a reaction which at least draws attention to the presence of the issue in the play, if not to the obliquity of its presentation.[15] The play has many references to saints, witches,

---

[14] Sceptical irony is deep in Shakespeare's tragic conception of *Othello*. The handkerchief signifies magic to Othello, whereas to Desdemona it is a precious token of his love. The strawberries on it have been seen by some critics as subliminally suggesting blood on a bedsheet – but representing loss of virginity or loss of life? Others have sensed allusion to the Catholic cult of sacred relics; but Iago makes a mockery of Othello's veneration of the object – to him it is a prop he can utilise in a web of deception. In *The Duchess of Malfi* when Antonio notices that his initials, embroidered on his handkerchief, have beene 'drowned in blood', his attempt to shrug it off as accident rather than omen is compromised by his concern for his child's horoscope which he has written out; and scepticism generally in the play is in tension with a whole code of omens and religious signs and images to which Webster grants undoubted affective force.

[15] The Italian spectator in 1618 was named Orazio Busino: see my account on p. xxxix. For an essay on *Othello* which has much relevance to *The Duchess of Malfi* in this respect see Robert N. Watson, '*Othello* as Protestant Propaganda', in Claire McEachern and Debora Shuger, ed., *Religion and Culture in Renaissance England* (Cambridge 1997), pp. 234–57; see also, more generally in this direction, Alison Shell, *Catholicism, Controversy and the English Literary Imagination, 1558–1660* (Cambridge 1999). Good essays may be found in Brian Morris, ed., *John Webster, Mermaid Critical Commentaries* (1970) and the list of 'Further Reading' below.

devils, omens, ghosts, presented sometimes as superstition, sometimes as apparently having real efficacy. A central concern in the play as a whole is with the opposed concepts fate / accident, substance / emptiness, at a historical moment when Christianity was in doctrinal crisis, cultural values seemed at hazard, when oblique perspectives were cultivated for their revealing insights.[16]

Narrative Direct and Oblique

The Duchess of Malfi begins with a conversation between two courtiers. It has an unhurried, almost casual air, as if the speakers had no particular business to attend to;[17] gradually the movement of persons on and off stage becomes busier as the scene progresses, and then it emerges that the important guests, the Cardinal and his brother Ferdinand, are preparing to depart; yet Webster scarcely makes this kind of information a priority for the audience: indeed it is only slowly and piecemeal that an audience gleans the fact that Antonio has just been chosen by the Duchess as her steward, or that an equestrian tournament has just finished, or – even later, almost at the end of Act I – that triumphs and feasts have been held; but precisely on what occasion, or for what duration, is left unclear.

Webster creates a court atmosphere of restless coming and going so that his exposition is indirect and oblique; it is all the more striking to discover that there is, nevertheless, a strong underlying design. This is evident in his use of Antonio and Delio in the first part of Act I. By keeping the pair continuously on stage, Webster provides through them, as anchormen, a series of perspectives: now he will advance them to deliver commentary, now move them to the side so that they observe and overhear either this pair, the Cardinal and Bosola, or that trio, Ferdinand and Castruchio and Silvio, or that other pair, Ferdinand and the Duchess. In this way Webster induces an audience to take an alert, critical interest in what they are shown: a succession of small groups composed by a permutation of individuals. From the beginning these people are all possessed by strong emotional drives and make a strong first impression, especially in their graphic comments on each other and on the central issue of good and bad government, but as the Act develops Webster involves an audience in reassessing and adjusting first impressions: they learn that they must observe, not merely listen: they must guess at motive, analyse character.

[16] See Ernest B. Gilman, *The Curious Perspective* (New Haven and London 1978).

[17] In performance it is sometimes made visually clear that Antonio has just come from the tilt-yard: as in Poel's 1892 promptbook. In 1960 at the Shakespeare Memorial Theatre, Stratford, Antonio entered hot and tired as if from jousting and wet his handkerchief in a fountain.

At last the Duchess herself enters, but Webster strictly controls the audience's important first impression of her: she is accompanied by the Cardinal and they stand clearly displayed to view – but the words the audience hear are not theirs but the onlooking Antonio's, and what he has to say is that the Cardinal is a villain as black as his brother Ferdinand, but their sister the Duchess is the very opposite: the three of them are like medals formed in the same mould but of quite different quality and temper, the Duchess is of the rarest purity; but since the remark comes from Antonio, who has shown a tendency to idealism, an audience may wonder whether he may not see things as more absolute than in reality they usually tend to be.

Notice that once Webster has established this form of attention in his audience he introduces an intenser focus, dispensing with the mediating on-stage observers altogether: Ferdinand's hiring of Bosola takes place on an otherwise empty stage, so does the menacing exchange when the brothers bid their sister farewell,[18] and finally it can be on a bare stage, completely alone, that the Duchess delivers a soliloquy.

Sex and Power: 'The spirit of greatness or of woman'

When the brothers take their leave of the Duchess they abruptly discard their masks: no more deferring to her status as prince, they confront her with open threats, progressively violent and nakedly explicit. As brothers they take it as their right to dominate their sister, as men to dictate to this woman: that she is of their princely blood is all the more reason for her to concede their authority over any alliance to be made by her marriage. They forbid her to marry. The Cardinal threatens that 'The marriage night / Is the entrance into some prison' and Ferdinand warns her even against thinking of it: 'Your darkest actions, nay, your privat'st thoughts, / Will come to light'. Ferdinand then physically threatens her with a dagger: when he identifies it as their father's dagger, the gesture symbolises incestuous passion, not just paternalistic power at its most naked. The Duchess is left alone. Whatever defiance there may be in her words, the stage image of the solitary woman suggests isolation, vulnerability.

---

[18] Since in Q1 Cariola's entry is simply part of a 'massed entry' at the head of the scene, editors of critical editions must choose where exactly to place it. Some editors have her enter with the Duchess at line 284 but I am convinced that it should not be until 341, so that the exchange between the brothers and the Duchess is in private. As Brown notes, the later entrance has the advantage that Ferdinand and the Duchess are alone when he says what he seems to have restrained until the Cardinal's departure.

Webster, having brought the dramatic rhythm to a climax on this note, and the stagecraft to rest on the motionless single figure, now switches to a very unexpected mood, one associated rather with romantic comedy and (ironically enough, here) with its elements of festive anarchy and reversal. The Duchess, as a widow but one no longer in submissive mourning, has full power over her dukedom and her court, power normally held by a man, and her male court is subject to her (this is one of several interesting parallels that suggest themselves to Shakespeare's *Twelfth Night*). By her command Antonio must come to take official instructions. She teases him, then sets out to woo and win him, thereby reversing the gender-roles in which the man takes the initiative in courtship. She also breaks the social and political constraints that require those of noble blood to marry their equals: Antonio's family is of inferior rank and he is also her servant, so that in marrying him the Duchess installs her servant as her lord and master.[19]

Webster puts the power structures in a fresh, defamiliarised light: the unusual sight of a woman wielding male privileges makes starkly apparent what the accepted structures are and how they work normally to privilege men – especially so when males are represented as so passionately hostile and oppressive as her brothers are here; and to see a man, Antonio, exposed to the social and cultural subjection commonly experienced by women, is to be confronted head-on with the issue of gender.[20] Antonio's subsequent career in the play exhibits progressive debilitation and enfeeblement. Later the Duchess is forcibly stripped of her dower, the duke-

---

[19] Later in III.ii.7–8 she calls him 'Lord of Misrule' and he replies 'Indeed, my rule is only in the night'. The Lord of Misrule presided at feasts and was chosen for his youth or low degree, inverting the normal hierarchy in the spirit of foolery, festive licence and anarchy. In this connection it is possible to make good sense of the suggestion (Inga-Stina Ekeblad, 'The 'impure art' of John Webster', *RES,* vol. 9 (1958)) that the masque of madmen in IV.ii is related to another festive custom, that of charivari, a mock-masque baiting the bride who married too soon after the death of her husband, or who made an unequal match: a ruffianly band showed their disapproval by making clamour and antic dances. More broadly, the use of masks in festivals is an ancient tradition formalised in comedy, where the temporary release from fixed, normal identity by wearing disguise, often in the form of fantastic masks, liberates repressed energies and effects positive transformation. Shakespeare gives concentrated attention to these elements in *Twelfth Night,* which is occasionally in Webster's mind in this play.

[20] Webster's presentation of the Duchess and her choice of a husband is much more complex than Painter's (Webster's source), who condemns the Duchess as a wanton widow. Webster, like Shakespeare in *Romeo and Juliet,* seems deliberately to take a more sympathetic view of his characters and of the significance of the story than he found in his source.

dom, by the Pope acting on her brothers' information against her; and with her dower goes her princely immunity.[21] Yet the Duchess must defiantly invert the normal master-servant relationship as a necessary precondition for creating a relationship of love, free from the alienating obligations of noble blood and the fetters of power politics. It is to be a union which (as can be seen from III.ii) prolongs the tender, happily flirtatious, witty relationship of courtship, although Webster's ironic design stresses that it is her pregnancies, the 'natural' fact of her female sexuality, that betray her.

She is seen to exercise her freedom as a prince, once to her own liking (choosing Antonio) but once to her brothers' liking (choosing Bosola). Displaying her power then lets the brothers penetrate her security. It seems a small thing but it is fatal: Ferdinand, on the point of leaving Malfi, requests a place for Bosola at her court and, perhaps with only the slightest hesitation, she agrees, then leads them off-stage: but as they go the Cardinal privately tells Ferdinand he is sure Bosola is the right man for a spy. The audience only minutes earlier has seen the Cardinal coldly rejecting Bosola, but now they learn that was all an act; and here, likewise, Ferdinand's request to the Duchess, far from being the afterthought it seemed, turns out to have been carefully plotted in advance and deftly performed.[22] This clearly shows how politically sophisticated and amoral the brothers are.

Duchess of Malfi she may be, spirited and defiant, young and beautiful: but if she wants to choose a husband her family disapprove of, it must be, as in *Romeo and Juliet*, in secret, and though she does protect that vital secret for a time she fails to conceal the birth of her children, and Antonio fails to conceal his sudden wealth. The results are bad enough – the discontent of her subjects and her own public humiliation as a prince (see III.i.24–37) and her husband's disgrace (III.ii.180–222) – it is only that they are insignificant compared to the horrifying events that follow – her own arrest, torture and murder, and the deaths of her children and Antonio.

Her brothers defy every rule and principle of good government and self-government, the Aragon family characteristic of wilfulness takes the form, in them, of extreme abuse of power, all negative and destructive in effect. Yet when the Duchess first shows spirit it is provoked by her brothers. She is Ferdinand's actual twin, and the

---

[21] Lisa Jardine, *Still Harping on Daughters* (1983), pp. 91–2.

[22] 'Sister I have a suit to you' might even have a subterranean sexual sense; and the Duchess, if she detects this and wants to deflect it, might think that accepting Bosola is the quickest way; but in deflecting the one intrusion she unwittingly allows another. A moment later the audience sees Bosola accept the contract from Ferdinand to be a spy.

Judi Dench (Duchess) and Richard Pasco (Antonio)
Royal Shakespeare Company 1971
(Photograph from The Shakespeare Centre Library,
Stratford-upon-Avon)

Cardinal too is obsessed by their consanguinity: to stress a close physical resemblance between all three, as was done in the RSC productions in 1971 and 1989, seems justifiable from Webster's text: to see in the Duchess a family likeness to, as well as an extreme difference from, her brothers, makes her less the alabaster saint, more the warm-blooded woman – and one conscious of her noble rank. She chooses one man, but hers is no simple domesticity. Only when at last alone with Antonio does she display tender and human warmth, though complicated by wit and awareness of riskily high stakes. Her proud Aragonian blood gives her the nerve to enter this labyrinth (her own metaphor), but unlike Theseus she lacks prudence, has no thread to find her way out again. As a prince she cannot – except at peril – resist political reality or her public role. The general assumptions of her society (as expressed in Webster's sources Belleforest and Painter[23]), let alone the ruthless machiavellianism prevailing in Italy's princedoms, mean that the Duchess is obliged to devise plots and practise deception: even in Act I when she tells her brothers she will never marry she has presumably already made her mind up to woo Antonio.

Deceit and spying are practised by the Duchess as well as by the Cardinal and Ferdinand. The audience will see that she is rebellious in choosing to marry, and especially to marry her social inferior, a steward, but – being a woman – she is doubly courageous, and it is thrilling to see her take on a whole cultural system. Webster is careful to show that she makes mistakes; one view of this is that her humane ideals fatally distract her, another that she is too proud and self-willed to take the game as seriously as do her opponents; another that being female and marrying means, inevitably, pregnancies, children: one may build in sonnets pretty rooms but Nature's law is change, not fixity. Hence, between the wooing of Act I and the fragile, happy, married flirtatiousness of Act III, Webster interposes so much anxious and nefarious activity: the clouds gather and the prospect darkens.

Act I presents the figure of the Duchess herself as young, beautiful, confident, articulate and witty, as opposed to her brothers' misogynistic invective and caricature, but Act II in sharp contrast presents insistently harsh images of woman's physicality, in the states of old age, heavy pregnancy, and sexual wantonness. First an Old Lady enters and Bosola subjects her to a cruelly satiric disquisition on ugliness, ageing and disease; then the Duchess as she enters has to make a small joke in acknowledgement of her own visibly increasing girth and heavy gait. Bosola has already detected physical signs that suggest pregnancy: 'she pukes, her stomach seethes, The fins of her eyelids look most teeming blue'. The diagnosis is

---

[23] See the discussion above, pp. xii–iv.

confirmed as the audience watch her eating – and eating surprisingly greedily – the apricots that Bosola gives her. She then starts to feel unwell and has to be helped off stage with the onset of labour pains. This is a graphic physical contrast to the poised and happy young woman who courted Antonio. Again the Old Lady (possibly the midwife) hurries over the stage and Bosola detains her, again insisting on ugly mockery of women's sexuality. Antonio confides to Delio that the Duchess is suffering 'the worst of torture, pain, and fear'. These events take place at night. Bosola in the darkness hears a woman's screams from the Duchess' lodgings. All this is calculated to make an audience anxious for the Duchess; her childbirth is presented not as a natural and happy part of love and marriage, but as agonising and very dangerous.

Webster concludes Act II by introducing a new female character, Julia, the Cardinal's mistress, in whom the concerns of Act II are fitly concluded. Julia is a complex parallel to the Duchess: she shamelessly lies to conceal her affair from her aged husband, the Duchess resorts to secrecy under duress, to conceal her marriage from her perverse brothers; both women boldly pursue their emotional lives and their sexual desire, and in doing so both have to be daring since they break strong social or moral taboos. In Julia there is a positive relish for danger, choosing a prince of the Church, and one so coldly cruel, yet those very reasons enhance erotic desire. It is possible to see the Duchess as enjoying a similar thrill in her dangerous choice of Antonio. Her brother the Cardinal, more coldly, uses Julia for his selfish pleasure then discards her sadistically,[24] whereas her other brother Ferdinand is slave to voyeurism and sexual paralysis, torturing himself with images of his nobly-born sister enjoying the grossest lusts of crude labourers, 'some strong-thighed bargeman'. The punishments Ferdinand imagines reflect an obsessive carnality all his own: with a perverse thrill he visualises their bodies

> Burnt in a coal pit with the ventage stopped,
> That their cursed smoke might not ascend to heaven;
> Or dip the sheets they lie in, in pitch or sulphur,
> Wrap them in't and then light them like a match   (II.v.67–70)

In the Duchess' case erotic desire harmoniously includes the humane and the maternal (although one should remember her bold wooing, and the erotic spice added by intimate banter in the pres-

[24] In the 1960 Shakespeare Memorial Theatre production Julia was red-wigged like the Duchess to make a visual parallel with her; this also implied in the Cardinal unrecognised incestuous tendencies towards his sister, and a close parallel between him and Ferdinand.

ence of Cariola, and by the frisson of the game of stealing out of the bedchamber in the dark). It is in the Duchess' brothers that sexual desire is distorted and wholly ugly, cruelty and danger essential erotic stimuli. In Julia erotic feeling is open and forthright: her seduction of Bosola at pistol-point (V.ii) suggests an interest in 'rough trade' but also contains echoes of the Duchess' wooing of Antonio in Act I. Julia too is spirited and impulsive, and she is prepared in Act V to take the sexual initiative. To secure Bosola's favours she takes a dangerous risk and an exciting one as she tries to trick the Cardinal, with Bosola a hidden voyeur.

Spying

By then surprise entrances from secret concealment have become almost the play's trademark and they are especially associated with Ferdinand. Immediately after presenting the death of the Duchess Webster shows first its shocking impact on Ferdinand, who enters promptly – because, presumably, he has been watching the whole time from concealment. It seems indeed plausible that he is to be imagined lurking constantly behind the door throughout the torments of the Duchess in Act IV. Yet, ironically, the first to employ spying as a tactic is the Duchess, for the final episode of Act I begins when Cariola brings Antonio to the Duchess then leaves the pair to play their scene apparently alone, but in fact (by the Duchess' direction) observes and overhears them from concealment; then, just at the point where Antonio and the Duchess agree, Cariola enters again – and this gives Antonio such a shock he cries out 'Ha'. Cariola also takes part in a subsequent spying episode (though again benevolently intended) in III ii, this time *with* Antonio *against* the Duchess, when the two of them steal out of the chamber as the Duchess gazes in her mirror.

Spying scenes are as memorably effective in comedy as in tragedy – as when in *Twelfth Night* Malvolio is spied on by the plotters as he reads the forged love-letter from Olivia, or in *The Winter's Tale* when jealous Leontes watches his pregnant queen Hermione take the hand of Polixenes; but perhaps the most famous Shakespearean spying is in *Hamlet*, where the activity is so frequent it constitutes a theatrical metaphor for the world of the play, with its secret heart of undiscovered murder buried in a treacherous court. Webster in *The Duchess of Malfi* likewise bases his plot on secrets – every character has a secret and many episodes in the play present spying or overhearing.

In V.iii Webster presents an extraordinary episode when Antonio and Delio visit a ruined abbey and graveyard. As they converse an echo is heard, on the face of it simply an acoustic effect of the ruined walls. The echo sounds to Antonio like the Duchess' voice, and the audience, like Delio, sees that the phrases which compose

Eric Porter (Ferdinand) and Peggy Ashcroft (Duchess)
Royal Shakespeare Company 1960
(Photograph from The Shakespeare Centre Library,
Stratford-upon-Avon)

the echoes could be construed, if connected, as a warning to Antonio.[25] The emphasis that Antonio's stricken state of mind makes him prey to delusions is important. Webster invented this scene, which is not in the sources, and his whole conception of it is ironic. There is irony at another level also, alluding to dramatic technique, for in this play so much depends on prefiguring and reflection, on pre-echoes and echoes.[26]

The scene develops, though to equivocal effect, a central theme, religious philosophy, with which the Duchess comforts Antonio at their final leave-taking: 'In the eternal Church, sir, / I do hope we shall not part thus' (III.v.69–70) and on which she meditates in her lowest point of dejection: 'Dost thou think we shall know one another / In th'other world?' (IV.ii.18–19). It is the hope for a country far beyond the stars, of which only dim images and echoes are sensed here, among the prisons and ruins where fearful mankind live, which animates the Duchess as she confronts her tormentors. As a counterpoint to the incoherence, confusion and horrors in which the play is to end, Antonio experiences, or dreams, a momentary reunion with his wife: then the vision fades, and night comes again.

Webster's Echo is to Delio an acoustic phenomenon, and questionable: indeed it is more questionable, being only a voice, than the ghost which in *Hamlet* returns from the 'undiscovered country' of death. The Duchess of Malfi returns (if one so interprets something so equivocal) not as a forbidding figure clad in armour demanding revenge but a feminine voice; and when one searches earlier in the play for a pre-echo of the scene, it turns out to be III.ii. One clue is the echoed phrase 'Never see thee more': this leads to others. The Echo scene is the reverse, as in a mirror, of the episode in III.ii where Antonio (with Cariola) watches helplessly from off-stage as on-stage the Duchess, gazing at her face in her mirror, is threatened

---

[25] Echo constitutes a metatheatrical allusion, and a bold one, alluding to Webster's own technique of construction, beyond being a conceit associating the Duchess with the story of Echo in Ovid, *Metamorphoses*. Webster perhaps modelled it on Shakespeare's in *The Winter's Tale*, when the figure Time is introduced abruptly to explain a jolting gap of sixteen years in the narrative.

[26] There are a number of such metatheatrical allusions through the play, perhaps the most memorable is the Duchess declaring 'I account this world a tedious theatre, / For I do play a part in't 'gainst my will' (IV.i.81–2). Later Ferdinand remarks to Bosola after the strangling: 'For thee – as we observe in tragedies / That a good actor many times is cursed / For playing a villain's part – I hate thee for't' (IV.ii.278–80); the last one being Bosola's remark that Antonio came by his death through a mistake such as he had 'often seen / In a play' (V.v.94–5). Bosola ultimately sees himself 'an actor in the main of all, / Much 'gainst mine own good nature' (V.v.84–5).

by Ferdinand[27] after which Antonio and Cariola return to comfort her. V.iii reverses this, with the Duchess-Echo off-stage anxious about the on-stage Antonio. Poignantly as the scene ends she can show herself – but only in a vision to Antonio, as a 'face folded in sorrow' (V.iii.44). It is more effective if the audience imagine it than if it is shown – although Webster may have intended a special visual effect.[28]

Death

We have seen how Webster emphasises the different perspectives from which the action can be viewed, and how easily misjudgements are made in interpreting what one overhears or sees. This applies even to death, which one would think appalling precisely for its certainty – as Ferdinand finds it to be on seeing the Duchess dead: 'Cover her face. Mine eyes dazzle. She died young' (IV.ii.254). The superbly memorable utterance and the arresting stage image combine to dominate an audience's imagination: it is so apparently conclusive an utterance, yet Webster subverts it only a moment later: for after Ferdinand has gone the Duchess will revive – like Juliet, like Desdemona, like Imogen. She was not in fact dead, and Ferdinand, for all his obsessively fascinated gaze, is deceived:[29] she returns to consciousness for a moment, and it is only after Bosola's comforting (if deceiving and false) words that she finally dies breathing the word 'mercy'.

---

[27] There is a visual allusion to the Dance of Death, where the figure of Death arrests men and women of various ages and ranks, including youthful queens and duchesses. The mirror in such cases is an emblem of female vanity.

[28] See the note to this line. Webster has avoided the clumsier melodrama of his previous tragedy where a ghost enters and as a sign of doom silently throws earth on Flamineo and shows him a skull (*The White Devil*, V.iv.120–37).

[29] It is almost as if Webster takes as his text Shakespeare's line 'There's no art / To find the mind's construction in the face' (*Macbeth*, I.iv.11–12). It is Ferdinand himself who asserts 'they whose faces do belie their hearts / Are witches' (I.i.302–3). Antonio's final sight of the Duchess is a vision of 'a face folded in sorrow' (V.iii.44). Early in Act I Bosola is angered at Ferdinand's suggestion that 'some oblique character' in his face made the Cardinal suspicious of him: Bosola retorts 'There's no more credit to be given to th'face / Than to a sick man's urine, which some call / The physician's whore, because she cozens him' (I.i.229–31). Later Bosola hides his face in a mask when arresting the Duchess. There are numerous other allusions to faces, whether like the Cardinal's, a toad-pool (I.i.154–5), or like Castruchio's, foolish (II.i.3), or the Old Lady's, painted, or the French lady's, flayed after the smallpox, or growing lean like Antonio's (III.i.9–10). Julia accuses Bosola of using love-powder, since nothing else could make her fall in love with 'such a face' (V.ii.154).

It is a grim intertwining of two insights that Webster contrives here, a destabilising of the belief that men can trust their own eyes and judgement, and at the same time a demonstration that drama is the mode of artistic discourse closest to – indeed mirroring – the real deceptive state of the world as men experience it. Webster's interest in this is most powerfully apparent in the sequence of events involving deception, from the frighteningly faceless masked men who arrest the Duchess in Act III to her death late in Act IV. The series of disguises and deceptions – the episode in darkness when Ferdinand gives her a severed hand, the traverse drawn to display her husband and children dead, the entry of the madmen – culminates in the entry of Bosola disguised as an old man to make the chilling announcement 'I am come to make thy tomb' and deliver a sermon:

> Thou art box of worm-seed, at best, but a salvatory of green mummy. What's this flesh? A little cruded milk, fantastical puff paste ... Didst thou ever see a lark in a cage? Such is the soul in the body[30] (IV.ii.118ff.)

Seen as a whole this sequence has a design, it figures the death of the Duchess in terms of an inverted wedding celebration. The madmen constitute an anti-masque and charivari (see fn. 19) – though these are real madmen, not fantastics artificially contrived to entertain King James I's court, and while they may provoke laughter in an audience they grimly suffer actual spiritual torture or mental disorder. As Bellman, Bosola gives her presents from her brothers – a coffin, cord and bell. The dirge is the exact inversion of an epithalamion or wedding-song; then follows the pronouncement of the death sentence, strangling; finally, according to this pattern, the noose is a wedding ring of death and the strangling a brutal act of destruction, the exact reverse of the ceremony of marriage itself.

The Duchess, however, exerts her will at the last and intervenes, choosing consciously to stage herself in an attitude of Christian devotion, kneeling at prayer: the addition of the rope round her neck might be given a different significance – an emblem of Christian martyrdom, not the instrument of deserved execution as Ferdinand intends. Recalling the dramatic narrative as a whole, an audience may recognise a silent, implicit parallel to the Duchess' wooing Antonio in Act I: there she raises Antonio *from* a kneeling position:

---

[30] Webster combines allusions to Shakespeare's Duke in *Measure for Measure* III.i. who advocates 'Be absolute for death' and to *King Lear* where Lear is reunited with Cordelia only to be imprisoned with her, but nevertheless cries joyfully 'Come let's away to prison: / We two alone will sing like birds i'th'cage' (V.iii. 8–9).

An early seventeenth-century English family tomb, at
Hambledon, Bucks: that of Sir Cope D'Oyley, his wife and
children. He died in 1633
(© Crown Copyright. NMR.)

> This goodly roof of yours is too low built,
> I cannot stand upright in't   (I.i.408–9)

Sensing that he is trembling, she urges that there is nothing to fear, *no* suggestion of death:

> This is flesh and blood, sir,
> 'Tis not the figure cut in alabaster
> Kneels at my husband's tomb   (I.i.445–7)

Now in Act IV on the point of death, the isolated Duchess takes heart, and treats the noose, the satiric-vengeful wedding ring of death, as a consummation devoutly to be wished – insisting it is the best gift she could possibly be given. Beside her the shrouded figure of Bosola, actual executioner-murderer, may double as symbol of Time and Mortality.

So much for the Christian symbolism; but not only is it equivocal in itself – as something consciously *played* – it is at once interpreted in a contrary sense by Cariola when she is dragged in. Cariola has hitherto expressed conventional respect for religion, protesting that the feigned pilgrimage is 'jesting with religion' (III.ii. 313–14) but ironically her reaction here is not veneration at a martyrdom, she sees only the corpse, strangled, of the woman she served. The audience will contrast her reaction to the Duchess' very different reaction when earlier she was shown the dead bodies of her husband and children – especially if the audience then also took the dead bodies for real, and shared something of the Duchess' shock. This recalls Shakespeare's late manner, in which the mystical and the strangely playful are mingled, as at the revival of Hermione in *The Winter's Tale* and the death of Cleopatra in *Antony and Cleopatra*.

Cariola's death, which immediately follows that of the Duchess, is only the first of a succession of contrastingly various deaths by which Webster echoes and mirrors what is evidently the play's key event, even if it is far from being in any sense its conclusion. This makes the play into a kind of *ars moriendi*,[31] a theatrical exploration of the Duchess' meditation

> I know death hath ten thousand several doors
> For men to take their exits   (IV.ii.209–10)

The dark paradox is that whereas in a story the ending completes

---

[31] See Forker, pp. 339–40; and for a detailed study of Webster's use of the *ars moriendi* tradition see Bettie Anne Doebler, 'Continuity in the Art of Dying: *The Duchess of Malfi*', in *Comparative Drama* 14 (1980), 203–15.

shape and meaning, in a life the ending is death, something obscure and indeterminate. The Cardinal contrives a mocking end for Julia by making her kiss a poisoned Bible, Bosola's sword-thrust in the dark strikes the wrong man, Antonio, the very one he vowed to save – 'Such a mistake as I have often seen in a play'. The Cardinal's epitaph from Bosola is that he ends 'in a little point, a kind of nothing' and Bosola's final conclusion is profoundly inconclusive:

> We are only like dead walls, or vaulted graves,
> That ruined, yields no echo.   (V.v.96–7)

The final words of the play offer what sounds like a clear conclusion:

> 'Integrity of life is fame's best friend,
> Which nobly, beyond death, shall crown the end'.

Yet even this is bedevilled by the ironic sting in the quotation's tail, for Horace later in the Ode also says that not even a wolf would attack a man possessed of integrity of life. Is the implication that the Duchess lacked integrity, since she died at the command of the wolf-man Ferdinand?

Webster makes the audience revise its sense of the play as a tragedy. At first sight it might be supposed that it is quite obvious – that as the title suggests, the tragedy is that the Duchess dies; but as Act IV proceeds it transpires that if the Duchess endures suffering, she is not finally broken by it, and that if her brothers and Bosola dispense suffering, it is reflected back on to them too, and that it is finally in them, not in their intended victim, that the torture ends in despair, a sense of inner void, 'a kind of nothing'.

The Play of Double Senses

A key to the play's exploration of paradox is Bosola, declared at the outset by Antonio to have goodness, although Delio recalls the rumour that he may have committed murder. Bosola himself sounds harsh enough for this in the first scene, his grotesque description of the Aragonian brothers – 'like plum trees that grow crooked over standing pools' – shades into a recognition of himself as just another parasite eager to feed on his hosts – he imagines himself hanging on the brothers' ears 'like a horse-leech till I were full, and then drop off'. When Ferdinand offers gold Bosola at first resists, or pretends to: the coins are 'devils, / Which hell calls angels': but then he caves in and takes the money – 'Thus the devil / Candies all sins o'er'. This is a man who followed an honourable service as a soldier by dishonourable civilian life as a secret agent; taking a step too far with murder, and having been brutalised in the galleys, he now

Bob Hoskins (Bosola) and Helen Mirren (Duchess)
Manchester Royal Exchange 1980
(© Photography by Kevin Cummins/Idols)

seems unlikely ever to retrieve either self-respect or control of his own life.

Ferdinand's new offer is a reward for corruption in the past as well as token of more to come. At least it brings with it the prestige and pay of a post in the Duchess' court. When Bosola does spy on the pregnant Duchess he seems to do it also out of a personal need to vent disgust at the female sex: his present of the apricots is a clever, sadistic variant on traditional jokes about a pregnant woman's longing for unusual foods at unusual times. He watches the Duchess eat the apricots and reacts with disgust. Telling her they were ripened in horse dung induces nausea in her but also reflects ironic contempt for himself, the supposedly loyal Master of the *Horse*.

This stance of disgust inclines towards the misanthropic, and so it is the more remarkable that once Bosola is obliged to make a closer relationship with the Duchess, an unexpectedly sympathetic, even tender, side of his nature appears. A similar split personality is apparent in Shakespeare's villain Iachimo in *Cymbeline*, who is committed to slandering the heroine's chastity and yet, when he sees her sleeping, is overwhelmed by her innocent beauty. In Act IV Bosola seems to have a function as Chorus when he reports that the Duchess in her imprisonment is so noble

> As gives a majesty to adversity:
> You may discern the shape of loveliness
> More perfect in her tears than in her smiles;
> She will muse four hours together, and her silence,
> Methinks, expresseth more than if she spake.   (IV.i.6–10)

While containing echoes from Sidney's *Arcadia* this offers a theatre audience a parallel to *King Lear*, the Gentleman's description of Cordelia's loving sorrow for her father's suffering,

> It seem'd she was a queen
> Over her passion ...
> patience and sorrow strove
> Who should express her goodliest. You have seen
> Sunshine and rain at once; her smiles and tears
> Were like a better way: (*King Lear,* IV.iii.13–14, 16–19)

In Jacobean revenge tragedies generally the figure of the malcontent is not just a hired contract-killer, he is given much more prominence and stronger motivation, interwoven in the drama's whole configuration. What is striking in Webster is that Bosola seems at the beginning a mere assassin; he is only gradually drawn towards the inner world of the heroine, his sense of righteousness and justice is revived by contact with her, but even so he still subjects her to persecution.

These inner contradictions in Bosola remain obscure, even if the audience is to imagine that Ferdinand maintains a hidden, threatening presence (back-stage, as it were) during the action of Act IV, forcing Bosola to carry out the torture. Ironically only the death of the Duchess gives him the resolution to convert to justicer. Though Bosola has a long-standing grievance against the Cardinal, it is nothing as severe as Vindice's, let alone Hamlet's. Bosola's relation to the Duchess shows in him something of the Janus-like doubleness of Iachimo; but Bosola's psychological torture of the Duchess to the point of death is more reminiscent of Iago. In III.v Bosola provokes the Duchess to a clear-eyed judgement of himself (and Webster's audience might recognise ironic echoes of *Othello* in the imagery):

> Thou dost blanch mischief,
> Wouldst make it white. See, see, like to calm weather
> At sea before a tempest, false hearts speak fair   (III.v.23–5)

Later Bosola tells the Cardinal and Ferdinand to their faces what he only dared say behind their backs in Act I: 'You have a pair of hearts are hollow graves' (IV.ii.309). Webster seems intent on developing Bosola as a complex, unstable figure undergoing real, violent inner change, though one unable to reform or destroy the system, it is too corrupted, power creates deceit everywhere – in Kafkaesque manner the system devours those who serve it. He is decidedly unpredictable and a source of tension because in his behaviour there is an alarming capacity to go beyond all normal limits. Contradiction and paradox are focused in Bosola, pressed to an irredeemable degree, a profound split.

The techniques of psychological torture are deployed to reduce the Duchess to despair, but her relationship to her torturer-inquisitor Bosola varies as he himself varies, by turns betrayer and confidant – destroyer, priest, psychiatrist. Her faith is tested until her physical endurance seems exhausted, while Bosola's own avowed nihilism is tempted to transform itself into faith by the Duchess' example, and vice-versa. By a mirror-process familiar in modern espionage and modern spy fiction, victim and interrogator are drawn together in a deep, dangerous, ambivalent intimacy. In the adoption of successive roles Bosola both performs and travesties Christian ritual, but whereas at death the Duchess adopts a fixed attitude of resolution by a supreme act of will, no such fixity or resolution applies in Bosola's case. In the 1980 Manchester production he died with a manic laugh.

As the Duchess is strangled an act of holy dying is performed on stage (if with self-conscious theatricality). Both in direct terms and by ironic parallel and allusion to earlier moments in the play, the figure of the Duchess has multiple significance – a daring lover vengefully destroyed, a monument, a martyr. She relives her marriage as the noose tightens, in her very submission she recovers her proud authority, she seems to make her destiny her choice – or is it just her proud Aragon blood that gives her the spirit to create a noble death if she is denied a noble life?

The Play on the Stage

In Webster's Lifetime

The title-page of the first edition of the play states that it was 'Presented priuatly, at the Black-/Friers; and publiquely, at the Globe' but it was published in 1623, some years later. Webster's The White Devil was published in 1612 and Webster worked on a successor, The Duchess of Malfi, but he had probably not completed the play when he wrote his Monumental Column (registered 25 December 1612 and published in 1613). The play had been performed by December 1614, because William Ostler, who first acted Antonio, died on 16 December 1614.

The Globe, an open amphitheatre playhouse on the south bank of the Thames, burned down on 29 June 1613 and it took over six months to rebuild, so possibly The Duchess of Malfi was first performed at the (Second) Blackfriars, an in-door playhouse, situated within the City itself. It held fewer spectators, no more than a third as many as the Globe,[32] and charged higher prices – a box beside the stage cost two shillings and sixpence, whereas at the Globe the top price was sixpence for a lords' room. Blackfriars was more easily accessible to the well-off and fashion-conscious, and to students at the Inns of Court; from the first its audiences included substantial numbers of ladies. The King's Men (probably from 1610) played at Blackfriars in winter (October to March or April, when the Court was in London and the law courts busy) and at the Globe in summer (when the Court was in the country and the law courts not in session). Citizens and their wives probably constituted the staple of Globe audiences, augmented by smaller but still significant numbers of gentlemen and their ladies, gallants and courtiers. The Blackfriars audience after 1610 became progressively more divergent in social composition from that at the Globe.[33]

Blackfriars performances were usually in the afternoon, though

---

[32] The Globe was capable of holding well over two thousand spectators; Gurr, Playgoing, p. 19, estimates an absolute upper limit of close to three thousand. Women comprised a significant proportion of the audience.

[33] But Gurr, Playgoing, p. 78, remarks that the division was 'more of social class than audience taste. That in turn implies that the price of admission had more effect than any class loyalty shown in the specific repertoires'.

some special performances were given at night: this indicates that the play and the auditorium could be lit artificially. Some lighting-effects, such as a darkening of the stage, might have been practicable at Blackfriars though not at the Globe,[34] but Webster utilises the simple conventions for indicating night which were customary in plays at the daylit amphitheatre playhouses – the bringing on of torches, candles or lanterns, augmented by emphasis on darkness in the dialogue. Night scenes represented in this way have an important place in such Globe plays as *Othello* and *Measure for Measure* written and acted before the King's Men acquired an indoor playhouse.

Music was a feature at Blackfriars: it was played before the play and between each Act. The five-Act structure of *The Duchess of Malfi* (where significant plot-time passes between the Acts) may have been intended to exploit this Blackfriars custom. Martin White, noting that contemporary references commend the quality of the Blackfriars orchestra, speculates that extensive use of music – both concordant and discordant – may have been used at Blackfriars to underpin the action of *The Duchess of Malfi*. Blackfriars had internal dimensions of 66 ft by 46 ft, probably including the stage and tiring-house.[35] (This is close to the size of the Cottesloe Theatre in today's National Theatre complex in London.) Although the Blackfriars stage was smaller than the Globe's it provided equivalent acting spaces 'above', and at stage level, where there were three entrances: the central one had a traverse curtain. Plays could be transferred without trouble from one playhouse to the other. The Blackfriars style of acting and speaking was probably more intimate than in the larger and open-air Globe – at Blackfriars the most expensive seats were closest to the actors, next to the stage, in the boxes and the stalls, whereas at the Globe the poorest patrons were closest to the stage, standing in the yard; the Globe's expensive seats were further away, in the gallery above stage-level. This probably indicates that the scale of performance at the two houses differed significantly. Indeed Martin White, who regularly experiments with performance in a reconstructed Jacobean indoor playhouse at the University of Bristol, believes that to have seen the same play at an outdoor and an indoor Jacobean playhouse would have been enormously dif-

---

[34] Argued by Martin White, *Renaissance Drama in Action* (1998), pp. 148–51. On lighting at Blackfriars see Keith Sturgess, *Jacobean Private Theatre* (1987), pp. 44–7, R. B. Graves, 'The Duchess of Malfi at the Globe and Blackfriars', *Ren.D* (1978), pp. 193–209. See also Alan Dessen, *Elizabethan Stage Conventions and Modern Interpreters* (1984).

[35] R. Hosley, 'The Second Blackfriars Playhouse (1596)', in C. Leech and T. W. Craik, eds., *The Revels History of Drama in English*, III (1975).

ferent experiences for spectators (letter of 29 September 1999). The King's Men were accustomed to playing in various places, at court[36] and on tour, and their technique, and their play-scripts, had to be adaptable.

In contrast to the highly exclusive and very occasional Jacobean Court Masque, in which Italian expertise in scenic theatre and lighting was, at great cost, copied, the repertory theatre of Shakespeare and his contemporaries was not scenic and those few large stage properties it did use had emblematic rather than realistic significance. Webster requires chairs of state, altars, shrines, tombs, and these would be brought on and off stage as required, and the 'waxwork' bodies would be shown by drawing the traverse curtain, upstage centre. Smaller properties in Webster are also important, constituting almost a visual summary of the story – most memorably the wedding-ring and the noose, the blood-spotted handkerchief, the dagger, the severed hand, and the 'waxwork' bodies; but significant use is also made of a jewel, gold coins, pen, ink and paper, apricots, horoscope, casket, mirror, pistol, pall, coffin, poisoned book. Costumes provided the opportunity for colour and display, but were also more precisely significant in a highly stratified society in which dress codes could closely identify the social class and occupation of a person – whether he be noble, as is Ferdinand, or merely the nobleman's doctor, whether she be a Duchess or only a lady, as is Julia. Clothes are made significant, as when Delio notes that Antonio is still dressed in the French style, or when the Duchess changes to a non-Italian style of loose-bodied gown to help conceal her pregnancy. Clothes are important when they are taken off, as when the Duchess removes jewels and prepares for bed, or when the Cardinal exchanges his religious robes for a soldier's armour. An Italian visitor to London, Orazio Busino, describes in 1618 a performance of a play he saw which was evidently *The Duchess of Malfi*; Busino says the players showed the Cardinal 'with a harlot on his knee'; he also says (apparently misunderstanding who Julia is) that the Cardinal was shown giving poison to one of his sisters. Clearly the robes of a cardinal always make a spectacular visual impact, and it is interesting that Busino sees the play as essentially a hostile presentation of Catholicism: 'all this was acted in condemnation of the grandeur of the church which they despise and which in this kingdom they hate to the death'. Busino evidently found the stage images impressive and memorable: 'first laying down his cardinal's habit on the altar, with the help of his chaplains, with great ceremoniousness; finally, he has his sword bound on and dons the soldier's sash with so much panache you could not imagine it better done'.[37]

[36] See John H. Astington, *English Court Theatre 1558–1642* (Cambridge 1999).
[37] Hunter, pp. 31–2.

The title-page of *The Duchess of Malfi* declares that the text restores cuts which the playing company had made because it was too long. Webster's published text is about a fifth longer than most Globe plays and two-fifths longer than most Blackfriars plays, although a number of Shakespeare plays are significantly longer than Webster's. In the theatre of the period, though the pace of playing was quick, performance time was well under three hours, so the cutting of Webster's text would be inevitable;[38] cuts might also be made, as they are today, for a small cast or to accommodate changes in the cast, or to avoid lengthy and elaborate spectacle, such as the dumb-show in Act III.

Webster does strikingly dignify the actors – he is the first in English to publish a list of the actors' names against their parts. This list probably dates from after a revival and close to the date of publication, 1623; it is not part of the original manuscript. In 1614 Burbage and Lowin were certainly leading members of the company, but the boys listed were probably too young then – Sharp was eleven or twelve, and Pallant nine. The role of the Duchess in 1614 may have been created by Richard Robinson. He later (in 1619) took over the role of Cardinal (created by Condell) to play opposite Taylor, the replacement Ferdinand. The Jacobean cast probably comprised fourteen to sixteen men and four boys, assuming some doubling.[39]

Bowdlerised and Adapted

Later seventeenth-century performances are recorded in 1630 at the Cockpit in Court, and after the Restoration – for the first time with women actors – by the Duke's company in 1662, 1668 and 1672, with Mrs Barry, the leading actress of the period, as the Duchess, and the great actor Betterton as Bosola. In 1708 Q4 was published, with changes probably reflecting the performance in 1707 at the Queen's Theatre in Haymarket. This text is significant for stage directions showing that the Doctor was played for laughs and that Bosola 'Starts' when he thinks he sees the ghost in V.ii. There is extensive cutting of bawdy – the beginning of the process of stage bowdlerisation which prevailed until the present century – and there are other longer cuts and silent omissions, Castruchio and the

---

[38] Sturgess, op.cit., p. 104, speculates on what might have been cut in Jacobean performances.

[39] Delio/Madman, Roderigo/Madman/Pilgrim, Grisolan/Madman/Pilgrim, Silvio/Doctor/Madman, Castruchio/Malateste/Madman. The assorted Servants, Officers, Churchmen, Guards, Executioners could have been acted by four to six hired men; the two older Children could have doubled as Lady and Old Lady – NCW, pp. 426–7.

Old Lady in II.i, the Loretto scene, III.iv, and most of Julia in V.ii.[40]
In 1733 at Covent Garden a stage adaptation by Theobald called
The Fatal Secret was presented. Here too Bosola was the role played
by the leading actor, Quin. The cuts extended to the Duchess'
wooing of Antonio, the apricot scene and all reference to childbirth,
also the Loretto scene, the dead hand, waxworks, and madmen.
Ferdinand repented and was presented with the Duchess' dead body
in a coffin, but in Act V (after the brothers accidentally killed each
other) Bosola revealed that the body in the coffin was a waxwork
and Antonio and the Duchess were still alive.

Further sentimental, simplistic and vulgarising adaptations were
still to come: in November 1850, at Sadler's Wells, Samuel Phelps
revived Webster's play as remodelled by R. H. Horne. Bosola was
made an uncomplicated villain. The Old Lady and Pescara were cut.
Julia was no longer the Cardinal's mistress but a court lady. The
narrative and dramatic structure was further reduced and simplified
to present a simple pious message: the Duchess was strangled off-
stage and then ran on to cry 'Mercy' and die, while a repentant
Ferdinand died with her name on his lips. Similar versions of the
play were performed over the next twenty-five years or so, using the
typical pictorial staging resources of the time. In an American production the Duchess appeared after her death in a cloud-bordered
heaven reunited with Antonio, while Ferdinand, on the stage below,
died repentant with her name on his lips.[41] William Poel, respon-
sible for important experiments with verse-speaking and Elizabethan stage conditions in productions of Shakespeare, showed no
equivalent respect in his production of *The Duchess of Malfi* (two
performances only) in 1892; he retained many routine cuts and
introduced further rearrangements of the text[42] and the dramatic
narrative to focus on the Duchess as a figure of passive religious
martyrdom. Poel did take an interest in torture, using drums,
strange sound effects and lighting; his dancing madmen were joined
by dancing women who turned their backs to appear as skeletons in
a dance of death.

Modern Productions

The Webster text was restored in a production (two performances
only) by the Phoenix Society at the Lyric Theatre, Hammersmith in
1919. A number of productions in the inter-war years followed,
among them that of Nugent Monck in 1922 and, most significantly,
of the Marlowe Society Cambridge (with George Rylands as the

---

[40] See Hunter, p. 25; NCW, pp. 428–30.

[41] NCW, pp. 46–7.

[42] Hunter, pp. 305–7, quotes some instructive samples.

Duchess) in 1924. Then in 1945 Rylands directed a successful West End production at the Haymarket Theatre, with a very strong Bosola (Cecil Trouncer) and a sensitive Duchess (Peggy Ashcroft). John Gielgud played Ferdinand, stressing the incestuous element in his obsession, a new and highly influential emphasis in stage interpretation. At that historical moment, the immediate aftermath of World War II, the play's grimness and violence were taken seriously and Webster's imaginative vision seemed to accord with current existentialism and post-Freudianism. Possibly the most successful production to follow was that at Stratford, Ontario in 1971, with Pat Galloway as the Duchess. She commanded a high style and yet expressed the tenderness and humour in the role. This production is also significant because it made Bosola the moral focus of the play, which lent coherence to Act V, so often a failure in modern stage productions – not only because Bosolas have had insufficient weight but also perhaps, as David Carnegie suggests, because the practice of cutting in the earlier part of the play weakens its structure.[43] In the same year, in Britain, Judi Dench presented a subtle, psychologically complex Duchess, 'with a talent for intrigue which comes out splendidly both in big scenes like the wooing of Antonio and in light throwaways, as where she skates over Bosola's traps with a graciously evasive smile. Also the part does grow from youthful confidence into an implacably stoical middle-age'.[44] This was perhaps the most intriguing and original interpretation of the role of Duchess in the whole period from 1945 to the present. Subsequent stage interpretations tend to resemble, in style and ideological bent, those in the far more frequent productions of Shakespeare's tragedies, for they often, in Britain, share the same directors, companies and leading actors. The bane of modern Shakespeare productions, elaborate and dominant sets, was supremely avoided in the 1980 Manchester production: inside the enormous old Corn Exchange the audience were arranged around a small open playing space, above which extended the vast, dark, echoing vault of the original building. This lent an added ominous significance to certain lines:

> Oh this gloomy world!
> In what a shadow, or deep pit of darkness,
> Doth womanish and fearful mankind live!   (V.v.99–101)

and it gave an ironic echo to Bosola's death-laugh.

---

[43] For a fuller account of the Canadian production see David Carnegie in NCW, pp. 436–7. PinP gives much useful information about cuts in the productions of the modern period.

[44] Irving Wardle, *The Times*, 16 July 1971.

In the 1985 National Theatre production, on the other hand, sets were obtrusive and distracted from the actors; Eleanor Bron's Duchess was felt to be insufficiently passionate, possibly because she played opposite a Bosola who was lightweight: and this may indicate a rule for any successful overall production of the play. Parallels are evident between the Bosolas of Bob Hoskins (1980) and Ian McKellen (1985), each of whom used humour to build a relationship with the audience but perhaps was too lightweight to enable his respective Duchess to achieve full tragic power. Parallels can also be drawn between the sensuous Duchess of Helen Mirren (1980) and that of Harriet Walter (1989). Harriet Walter has since written very intelligently about the play and her part in it – hers is indeed one of the most interesting pieces of recent commentary on Webster's play.[45]

A Summary of the Plot

The Duchess of Malfi is a widow, but still young. She has two brothers – Ferdinand, who is her twin, and the Cardinal. Visiting her in Malfi they warn her to remain chaste and unmarried. Antonio, a gentleman newly returned from France, has just been chosen by the Duchess as her steward. Bosola, a discontented soldier who has served the Cardinal, is chosen (at Ferdinand's request) by the Duchess as Master of Horse, but he serves the brothers as a spy. She secretly woos and marries Antonio.

Almost a year passes between Acts I and II. In Act II Bosola suspects the Duchess of being pregnant and gives her a present of apricots; these precipitate the birth of her child, an event which Bosola discovers and reports to the brothers. He does not discover the identity of the father. Antonio, fearing Bosola may be a spy, sends his friend Delio to Rome to discover what he can. When Ferdinand receives from Bosola the news about the Duchess' child he reacts with extravagant passion and violently vows revenge; the Cardinal displays rage too, but his is cold (II.v).

Despite their frustration the brothers do nothing in the gap of two to three years that intervenes between Act II and Act III. When Act III begins the Duchess has had two more children; Ferdinand has just arrived at her court. He suggests that the Duchess choose Count Malateste as a husband; she is evasive. Bosola informs Ferdinand of her additional children and Ferdinand resolves to visit the Duchess by night to extort a confession. The Duchess is seen (III.ii) preparing for bed in the company of Antonio and her servant Cariola. They

---

[45] See White, op.cit., pp. 88–100. White also has some useful remarks on the grotesque elements in the play as interpreted in modern stage production.

play a trick on her, stealing out of the chamber without her notic-
ing. Suddenly Ferdinand appears, and gives her a dagger with the
words 'Die then, quickly'. He threatens her unseen lover with death
and disappears again into the dark. Only then does Antonio – armed
with a pistol – return with Cariola, having observed the event from
concealment. The Duchess decides that Antonio must leave at once.
This is explained to the court as his dismissal for false stewardship.
The Duchess confides in Bosola – a mistake, as Bosola at once
informs Ferdinand. The Duchess sets out (at Bosola's suggestion) on
a pilgrimage to Loretto as a cover for her flight to Ancona where she
will join Antonio. In Loretto (III.iv) the Cardinal in dumb-show
exchanges his religious robes for the arms of a soldier: he banishes
the Duchess and her family and removes her wedding ring. The
Duchess receives a threatening letter from Ferdinand and decides
that she and Antonio must part. She sends him with their eldest son
to Milan. A party of masked men (their leader Bosola) arrest the
Duchess and take her with her children to her palace of Malfi.

Act IV begins with Ferdinand making another night visit to the
Duchess. He gives her a dead man's hand. Then Bosola draws a curtain to show her children and husband dead. Ferdinand returns and
the audience (but not the Duchess) learn that the figures were not
real but wax, intended to reduce her to despair. In IV.ii a group of
madmen are sent to the Duchess, after which Bosola, now disguised
as an old man, speaks of the futility of life and shows her a present
from her brothers: a coffin, cords and a bell. The Duchess, after
prayer, kneels and is strangled. Cariola is shown the body and
reacts in terror. She is strangled. Ferdinand enters and views the
body of the Duchess. The strangled bodies of the children are
shown. Ferdinand shows signs of incipient madness and lycanthropia, refusing Bosola any reward. Ferdinand leaves, then the
Duchess stirs, speaks again, twice, then finally dies. Bosola carries
her body out.

Act V begins, as did Acts I and III, with Antonio and Delio in
conversation. Antonio hopes for reconciliation with the Duchess'
brothers, he does not yet know that the Duchess is dead. He
resolves on a night visit to the Cardinal. In V.ii Ferdinand is completely mad, trying to strangle his own shadow. His doctor cannot
tame him. The Cardinal orders Bosola to kill Antonio. Julia, the
Cardinal's mistress, demands at pistol point that Bosola become her
lover. She offers to discover the cause of the Cardinal's melancholy
while Bosola observes from concealment. The Cardinal tells her
that he has had the Duchess and her children strangled but makes
her kiss a poisoned book. Bosola, too late, intervenes. Julia dies.
The Cardinal gives Bosola his key and orders him to bring the body
at midnight. Bosola in a soliloquy resolves to protect Antonio and
join him in his just revenge. V.iii is a conversation between Antonio

and Delio; a ruined cloister gives echoes which have ominous apt-
ness. V.iv begins with the Cardinal's command to the courtiers to
ignore any strange noises from his apartments during the night. The
Cardinal's soliloquy, in which he decides to have Bosola killed, is
overheard by Bosola who then stands aside as Ferdinand passes by.
When another figure enters in the darkness Bosola strikes with his
sword, but it is Antonio. Bosola speeds Antonio's death by telling
him his wife and children are dead. He directs the servant to remove
the dead body.

The final scene, V.v, shows the Cardinal trapped in his apartments by Bosola. Despite his cries for help he is stabbed to death;
Ferdinand, stark mad, enters at the last moment to wound the
Cardinal and in the scuffle fatally wounds Bosola before Bosola kills
him. The courtiers enter to hear the dying Bosola tell that revenge
is complete. Delio enters with the young son of Antonio, declaring
his hope to establish the boy in his 'mother's right'.

Note on the Text

This New Mermaid critical edition is based on a fresh analysis of
the first quarto of 1623, the only authoritative edition; my copy-
text is the British Museum copy of Q1, shelf-mark 644.f.72, col-
lated with the principal subsequent editions. Q1 exists in one
uncorrected and two corrected states, designated Q1a, Q1b and
Q1c. The second corrected state is found only in sheet G, outer
forme. Several press variants are clearly alterations not corrections;
the indications are that the author made them and several other
additions which are printed in the margins of Q1. Modernisation is
according to the conventions of the New Mermaid series. The col-
lation indicates all substantial emendations of the copy-text, variants which are not adopted but are of some interest, and changes in
copy-text lineation. Where necessary there are textual notes in the
Commentary. I have added stage directions (indicated by square
brackets) wherever they are essential to provide a performable version of the text, and in the same spirit I have modernised punctuation, using as light a touch as possible. Single quotation marks are
used for *sententiae*, as at II.iii.53–4.

Brown argued convincingly that Q1 was set by formes, not
seriatim, and by two compositors; NCW (pp. 451–2) provide an
analysis of punctuation patterns to further strengthen this hypoth-
esis. The printers' copy, as Brown argued, was virtually certainly
a scribal transcript by Ralph Crane – it has group entries for the
characters at the head of each scene, very few and inadequate
stage directions, and heavy punctuation. These features do not
correspond to those in Q1 of Webster's *The White Devil* which

almost certainly was set from Webster's manuscript, whereas they do correspond to Crane's practice as a professional scribe elsewhere. There are other characteristics in Q1 of *The Duchess of Malfi* which suggest Crane: the heavy use of parentheses and of a terminal colon especially in short dialogue lines, the habit of not beginning verse lines with a majuscule, the unusual use of the hyphen, the use of italic script for headings, songs, letters, titles and proper nouns. Crane intervened in many ways when transcribing dramatic texts, and T. H. Howard-Hill, *Ralph Crane and Some Shakespeare First Folio Comedies* (1972), concludes that Crane's habits seriously affect the authority of texts printed from his transcripts. The absence of profanities in the play, first noted by G. P. V. Akrigg, contrasts with *The White Devil* which has twenty-four uses of 'God' against *The Duchess of Malfi's* none. A Jacobean statute (3 Jac. I) forbade profanities so it is probable the playhouse manuscript (the copy Crane probably used in making his transcript) was censored, substituting 'Heaven' for 'God' – as at III.v.79–80.

ABBREVIATIONS

Alexander	Sir William Alexander, *The Alexandraean Tragedie*, in *The Monarchicke Tragedies* (1607)
Boklund	Gunnar Boklund, *'The Duchess of Malfi': Sources, Themes, Characters* (Cambridge, Mass. 1962)
Brennan	Elizabeth Brennan, ed., *The Duchess of Malfi*, The New Mermaids, 3rd edition (London 1993)
Brown	John Russell Brown, ed., *The Duchess of Malfi*, Revels Plays (London 1964)
Chapman	Allan Holaday, ed., *The Plays of George Chapman: The Tragedies* (Cambridge 1987)
Dent	R. W. Dent, *John Webster's Borrowing* (Berkeley and Los Angeles 1960)
E in C	*Essays in Criticism*
Florio	See Montaigne below
Forker	Charles R. Forker, *Skull Beneath the Skin: The Achievement of John Webster* (Carbondale 1986)
Gurr, *Playgoing*	Andrew Gurr, *Playgoing in Shakespeare's London* (Cambridge 1987)
Hunter	G. K. and S. K. Hunter, eds., *Penguin Critical Anthologies, John Webster* (Harmondsworth 1969)
Lucas	F. L. Lucas, ed., *The Complete Works of John Webster* (London 1927)
MLR	*Modern Language Review*
Montaigne, *Essayes*	Michel de Montaigne, *The essayes or morall, politike and millitarie discourses*, trans. J. Florio (1603)
NCW	David Carnegie, D. C. Gunby and Antony Hammond, ed., *The Works of John Webster* (Cambridge 1995)
N&Q	*Notes and Queries*
OED	*Oxford English Dictionary*
PinP	Kathleen McLuskie and Jennifer Uglow, ed., *The Duchess of Malfi*, Plays in Performance (Bristol 1989)
Pliny	(Caius Plinius secundus), *The historie of the world*, trans. P. Holland (1601)
Ren.D	*Renaissance Drama*
RES	*Review of English Studies*
RSC	Royal Shakespeare Company
SEL	*Studies in English Literature*
Shakespeare	G. Blakemore Evans, ed., *The Riverside Shakespeare* (Boston 1974)
Sidney, *Works*	A. Feuillerat, ed., *The Complete Works of Sir Philip Sidney*, (Cambridge 1912–26)

Tilley   M. P. Tilley, *A Dictionary of the Proverbs in England in the Sixteenth and Seventeenth Centuries* (Ann Arbor 1950)

The White Devil, *The Revenger's Tragedy*, *The Malcontent*, *The Changeling*, are cited from The New Mermaid editions.

- ed.   editorial emendation
- Q1   the quarto of 1623 (Q1a uncorrected, Q1b corrected, Q1c second corrected, sheet G outer forme only)
- Q2   the quarto of 1640
- Q3   the quarto of 1678
- Q4   the quarto of 1708
- s.p.   speech prefix
- s.d.   stage direction

FURTHER READING

Editions
F. L. Lucas, ed., *The Complete Works of John Webster* (1927)
John Russell Brown, ed., *The Duchess of Malfi*, Revels Plays (1964)
Elizabeth Brennan, ed., *The Duchess of Malfi*, The New Mermaids (1964 – 3rd ed. 1993)
David Carnegie, D. C. Gunby and Antony Hammond, ed., *The Works of John Webster* (Cambridge 1995)

Staging
David Bergeron, 'The wax figures in *The Duchess of Malfi*', *SEL* 18 (1978), pp. 331–9
R. B. Graves, '*The Duchess of Malfi* at the Globe and Blackfriars', *Ren.D* (1978), pp. 193–209
Andrew Gurr, *Playgoing in Shakespeare's London* (Cambridge 1987)
Keith Sturgess, *Jacobean Private Theatre* (1987)
Kathleen McLuskie and Jennifer Uglow, ed., *The Duchess of Malfi*, Plays in Performance (Bristol 1989)
Martin White, *Renaissance Drama in Action* (1998)

Critical Studies
Rupert Brooke, *John Webster and Elizabethan Drama* (1916). A pioneering study.
Inga-Stina Ekeblad, 'The 'impure art' of John Webster', *RES* vol. 9 (1958)
Norman Rabkin, ed., *Twentieth-Century Interpretations of 'The Duchess of Malfi'* (1968)
G. K. and S. K. Hunter, ed., *Penguin Critical Anthologies, John Webster* (Harmondsworth 1969)
Brian Morris, ed., *John Webster, Mermaid Critical Commentaries* (1970)
J. W. Lever, *The Tragedy of State* (1971)
M. C. Bradbrook, *John Webster, Citizen and Dramatist* (1980)
Lee Bliss, *The World's Perspective: John Webster and the Jacobean Drama* (1983)
Lisa Jardine, *Still Harping on Daughters* (Brighton 1983)
Charles R. Forker, *Skull Beneath the Skin: the Achievement of John Webster* (Carbondale 1986)
Christina Luckyj, *A Winter's Snake: Dramatic Form in the Tragedies of John Webster* (1989)
Dymphna Callaghan, *Women and Gender in Renaissance Tragedy* (1989)

Robert N. Watson, 'Tragedy', in A. R. Braunmuller and Michael Hattaway, ed., *The Cambridge Companion to English Renaissance Drama* (1990), pp. 301–51

Susan Zimmerman, ed., *Erotic Politics: Desire on the Renaissance Stage* (1992)

Brian Gibbons, *Shakespeare and Multiplicity* (Cambridge 1993). Chapter 3 discusses the staging of death.

Michael Neill, *Issues of Death: Mortality and Identity in English Renaissance Tragedy* (Oxford 1997)

Original title page

privately ... Blackfriars The Blackfriars Theatre, a smaller, in-door public play-house ('private' alludes to its select fashionable ambitions) which had been home to a company of boy-actors until it was taken over by the most famous and successful adult acting company, The King's Men, whose base was The Globe Theatre. From 1610 The King's Men performed concurrently in both houses.

publicly at the Globe The Globe, a large open amphitheatre-type playhouse ('public' for popular) on Bankside, was erected in 1599 with timbers transferred from the old Theatre in Shoreditch. The Globe burned down on 29 June 1613 (before the supposed date of the first performance of *The Duchess of Malfi*) and a more elaborate second Globe was built on the site; it was in use by June 1614. On the possible implications, for styles of performance, of the differences between The Globe and Blackfriars, see the Introduction pp. xxxvii–ix.

perfect and exact coppy What is really striking is this emphatic claim to present the author's fuller text, restoring the cuts made by the players for performance. It is Webster's dignity as author, not merely playwright, and of his work as literature, not as acting-script, that is given emphasis, and this is further stressed in the epigraph from Horace, in the dedicatory epistle where Webster asserts the enduring worth of his work, and the commendatory verses from fellow authors who stress the established fame of Webster and his Duchess.

Hora ... mecum Horace, *Epistles*, I vi 67–8: *Si quid novisti rectius istis, candidus imperti; si non, his utere mecum* ('If you know something better than these precepts, be kind and tell me; if not, practice mine with me'). As Lucas suggests, Webster presumably intends to apply this in the sense 'If you know a better play, let's hear it; if not, hear mine'.

THE
TRAGEDY

OF THE DVTCHESSE
Of Malfy.

As it was Presented priuatly, at the Black-
Friers; and publiquely at the Globe, By the
Kings Maiesties Seruants.

The perfect and exact Coppy, with diuerse
things Printed, that the length of the Play would
not beare in the Presentment.

VVritten by *John Webster.*

Hora.———*Si quid*———
———*Candidus Imperti si non his vtere mecum.*

LONDON:

Printed by NICHOLAS OKES, for IOHN
WATERSON, and are to be sold at the
signe of the Crowne, in *Paules*
Church-yard, *1 6 2 3.*

DEDICATION

To the right honourable George Harding, Baron Berkeley
of Berkeley Castle and Knight of the Order of the Bath to
the illustrious Prince Charles.

My Noble Lord,
That I may present my excuse why, being a stranger to your   5
Lordship, I offer this poem to your patronage, I plead this
warrant: men who never saw the sea yet desire to behold
that regiment of waters, choose some eminent river to guide
them thither, and make that, as it were, their conduct or
postilion; by the like ingenious means has your fame arrived   10
at my knowledge, receiving it from some of worth who,
both in contemplation and practice, owe to your honour
their clearest service. I do not altogether look up at your
title, the ancientest nobility being but a relic of time past,
and the truest honour indeed being for a man to confer   15
honour on himself: which your learning strives to propa-
gate, and shall make you arrive at the dignity of a great
example. I am confident this work is not unworthy your
Honour's perusal: for by such poems as this, poets have
kissed the hands of great princes and drawn their gentle   20
eyes to look down upon their sheets of paper, when the
poets themselves were bound up in their winding-sheets.
The like courtesy from your Lordship shall make you live in
your grave, and laurel spring out of it, when the ignorant
scorners of the Muses, that like worms in libraries seem to   25
live only to destroy learning, shall wither, neglected and
forgotten. This work, and myself, I humbly present to your
approved censure, it being the utmost of my wishes to have
your honourable self my weighty and perspicuous com-
ment; which grace so done me, shall ever be acknowledged   30
                              By your Lordship's
                                in all duty and
                                    observance,

                                John Webster.

1 *George Harding* Thirteenth Baron Berkeley (1601–58) the son and grandson of
  Lords Hunsdon who had been patrons of the Chamberlain's Men, the acting
  company honoured in May 1603 by royal patronage and thereafter re-named the
  King's Men (the King's Majesty's Servants).
9 *conduct* conductor   28 *approved censure* seasoned judgement

COMMENDATORY VERSES

In the just worth of that well deserver
Mr John Webster, and upon this masterpiece of tragedy.

In this thou imitat'st one rich and wise
That sees his good deeds done before he dies.
As he by works, thou by this work of fame
Hast well provided for thy living name.
To trust to others' honourings is worth's crime,
Thy monument is raised in thy lifetime,
And 'tis most just: for every worthy man
Is his own marble, and his merit can
Cut him to any figure, and express
More art than death's cathedral palaces
Where royal ashes keep their court. Thy note
Be ever plainness, 'tis the richest coat.
Thy epitaph only the title be,
Write 'Duchess': that will fetch a tear for thee,
For whoe'er saw this Duchess live and die
That could get off under a bleeding eye?

In Tragaediam.

Ut lux ex tenebris ictu percussa Tonantis,
Illa, ruina malis, claris fit vita poetis.

Thomas Middletonus,
Poeta & Chron:
Londiniensis.

In Tragaediam ... poetis To tragedy. As light springs from darkness at the stroke
of the thunderer, / May it (ruin to evil) be life for famous poets.
Chron: Londiniensis Chronologer of London. Thomas Middleton the playwright
was appointed to this post in 1620.

4

To his friend Mr John Webster
Upon his *Duchess of Malfi.*

I never saw thy Duchess till the day
That she was lively bodied in thy play:
Howe'er she answered her low-rated love,   5
Her brothers' anger did so fatal prove;
Yet my opinion is, she might speak more,
But never, in her life, so well before.

Wil. Rowley.

To the reader of the author,   10
and his *Duchess of Malfi.*

Crown him a poet, whom nor Rome nor Greece
Transcend in all theirs, for a masterpiece
In which, whiles words and matter change, and men
Act one another, he, from whose clear pen   15
They all took life, to memory hath lent
A lasting fame to raise his monument.

John Ford.

4 *bodied* embodied
5–6 *Howe'er ... prove* However eloquently in her real life the Duchess may have
   defended that misalliance which her brothers' anger made so fatal (Lucas).
7 *speak* have spoken
8 *But ... before* She can never have spoken so well as in your play (Lucas)
9 *Wil. Rowley* A dramatist who collaborated at various times with Webster,
   Middleton and Ford.
14–15 *whiles ... Act* while literature has its fashions and the theatre lasts (Brown)

The Actors' Names

Bosola, *J. Lowin.*
Ferdinand, 1 *R. Burbidge.* 2 *J. Taylor.*
Cardinal, 1 *H. Cundaile.* 2 *R. Robinson.*
Antonio, 1 *W. Ostler.* 2 *R. Benfield.*
Delio, *J. Underwood.*
Forobosco, *N. Towley.*
Malateste.
The Marquis of Pescara, *J. Rice.*
Silvio, *T. Pollard.*
The several mad-men, *N. Towley, J. Underwood, etc.*
The Duchess, *R. Sharpe.*
The Cardinal's Mistress, *J. Tomson.*
The Doctor, ⎫
Cariola,   ⎬ *R. Pallant.*
Court Officers.
Three young Children.
Two Pilgrims.

This list was printed in the first edition. No previously published English play has a cast list.

1 *R. Burbidge.* 2 *J. Taylor.* This indicates that the first-named was in the original performance (before Ostler's death on 16 Dec 1614) and the second in a revival some time after the death of Burbage on 13 March 1619.

Forobosco He has no lines to speak and is only referred to in II.ii.31. Perhaps this is a 'ghost' character – Webster altered his original plan in the course of composition and cut the part but forgot to delete the name from this list – or the part may have been cut in the acting version with Webster's assent – or perhaps without it, in which case its omission from the printed version is an oversight.

Three young Children The eldest a boy, the middle child a girl, the youngest a babe in arms (see III.v.82: 'sweet armful') presumably represented by a property doll.

[DRAMATIS PERSONAE]

FERDINAND, *Duke of Calabria, twin brother of the Duchess*
CARDINAL, *their brother*
BOSOLA, *formerly served the Cardinal, now returned from imprisonment in the galleys; then Provisor of Horse to the Duchess, and in the pay of Ferdinand*
ANTONIO, *household steward to the Duchess, then her husband*
DELIO, *his friend, a courtier*
CASTRUCHIO, *an old lord, Julia's husband*
SILVIO, *a courtier*
RODERIGO, *a courtier*
GRISOLAN, *a courtier*
PESCARA, *a marquis*
MALATESTE, *a count*
DOCTOR
DUCHESS OF MALFI, *a young widow, later Antonio's wife, and the twin sister of Ferdinand and sister of the Cardinal*
CARIOLA, *her waiting-woman*
JULIA, *wife of Castruchio and mistress of the Cardinal*
OLD LADY
TWO PILGRIMS
The Duchess' Children – *two boys and a girl*
Eight Madmen: *an astrologer, a lawyer, a priest, a doctor, an English tailor, a gentleman usher, a farmer, a broker*
Officers, Servants, Guards, Executioners, Attendants, Churchmen, Ladies-in-Waiting]

CASTRUCHIO The name Castruccio is in Painter who (following Belleforest) thus refers to Petrucci, Cardinal of Siena. Lucas suggests Webster saw it as a suitable name for Julia's old husband because it sounds as if it means 'castrated'. Florio defines the Italian word *castrone* as 'a gelded man ... a cuckold'.

CARIOLA Florio lists the Italian word *carriolo* or *carriuola* as (among other things) a 'trundle-bed'. In an age when personal servants slept in trundle-beds close to their employers, this name would be apt.

The Duchess' Children In III.iii.67 there is reference to a son by her first husband; the boy is called Duke of Malfi. This is possibly a 'ghost character' unless it is he who is referred to at V.v.111–12, although Ferdinand's assertion at IV.ii.273–5 seems incompatible with his existence; see also Pescara's remarks at V.v.105–7.

7

known many travel far for it, and yet return as arrant
knaves as they went forth, because they carried themselves
always along with them.

[*Exit* CARDINAL]

Are you gone? Some fellows, they say, are possessed with
the devil, but this great fellow were able to possess the   45
greatest devil and make him worse.

ANTONIO
He hath denied thee some suit?

BOSOLA
He and his brother are like plum trees that grow crooked
over standing pools: they are rich, and o'erladen with fruit,
but none but crows, pies and caterpillars feed on them.   50
Could I be one of their flatt'ring panders, I would hang on
their ears like a horse-leech till I were full, and then drop
off. I pray leave me. Who would rely upon these miserable
dependences, in expectation to be advanced tomorrow?
What creature ever fed worse than hoping Tantalus? Nor   55
ever died any man more fearfully than he that hoped for a
pardon? There are rewards for hawks and dogs when they

40–3 *I have ... them* A contradiction of the proverb that travel broadens the mind:
　　Webster is recalling Montaigne, *Essayes*, I.xxxviii, p. 119.

41 *arrant* thorough

49 *standing* stagnant

50 *pies* magpies

51–2 *hang ... full* I would feed them fulsome words of praise until I was sated by
　　their fat rewards (*horse-leech* = blood-sucker)

54 *dependences* the condition of living on promises

55 *Tantalus* The type of the disappointed man (hence the verb 'tantalise'), punished
　　in Hades by perpetual thirst, though up to his neck in water, and by hunger,
　　though fruit hung just beyond his grasp.

56 *died* (Q1b; did Q1a)

57 *pardon* (Q1b; pleadon Q1a)
　　dogs ed. (dogges, and Q1)
　　hawks and dogs In Q1 there is a space at the line-end after *hawkes, and dogges,*
　　and　　whereas the preceding and succeeding lines are printed full out right.
　　Presumably Q1's second *and* is an erroneous repetition. Lucas suggests the noun
　　horses had dropped out, but type could not have fallen out without movement –
　　indeed disintegration – of the whole page of type (as NCW note). The parallel in
　　Montaigne, *Essayes*, II.xii, p. 266, is inconclusive: it is true that the first part
　　does refer to men serving better, and for less entreaty, 'then wee vse vnto birdes,
　　vnto horses, and vnto dogges' – but then follows the second: 'We share the
　　fruites of our prey with our dogges and hawkes, as a meede of their paine and
　　reward of their industry': here 'horses' are omitted.

have done us service, but for a soldier that hazards his
limbs in a battle, nothing but a kind of geometry is his last
supportation.   60

DELIO
Geometry?

BOSOLA
Ay, to hang in a fair pair of slings, take his latter swing in
the world upon an honourable pair of crutches, from hospital to hospital. Fare ye well sir; and yet do not you scorn
us, for places in the court are but like beds in the hospital,   65
where this man's head lies at that man's foot, and so lower,
and lower.   [*Exit*]

DELIO
I knew this fellow seven years in the galleys
For a notorious murder, and 'twas thought
The Cardinal suborned it. He was released   70
By the French general, Gaston de Foix,
When he recovered Naples.

ANTONIO   'Tis great pity
He should be thus neglected, I have heard
He's very valiant. This foul melancholy
Will poison all his goodness, for, I'll tell you,   75
If too immoderate sleep be truly said
To be an inward rust unto the soul,
It then doth follow, want of action
Breeds all black malcontents, and their close rearing,
Like moths in cloth, do hurt for want of wearing.   80

[*Enter* CASTRUCHIO, SILVIO, RODERIGO *and* GRISOLAN]

---

65 *like* ed. (likes Q1)
71 *Foix* ed. (*Foux* Q1); Q1's *Foux* is probably a transcription error since the cor-
     rect form of the name appears in Painter. Historically, Gaston de Foix was still
     a child in 1501 when Naples was recovered.
72–80 Antonio apparently contradicts his previous remarks about Bosola at 22–28.
78–80 Malcontents, having been reared in secret (like moths in cloth) are able to do
     damage precisely because of the lack of activity (NCW).
80 s.d. ed. (SCENA II. / *Antonio, Delio, Ferdinand, Cardinall, Dutchesse,
     Castruchio, Siluio, Rodocico, Grisolan, Bosola, Iulia, Cariola.* Q1)
     Some editors mark an exit for Antonio and Delio, only to make them enter again
     immediately, when they have to resume their conversation. This seems too
     clumsy, and it is probable Webster intended no scene break but that they should
     stand aside to observe the courtiers. Probably, as NCW suggest, the scribe saw
     a s.d. for several characters and assumed a scene break, which he marked, fol-
     lowing this with a massed entry collecting all the characters indicated in subse-
     quent s.d.'s.

DELIO
  The presence 'gins to fill. You promised me
  To make me the partaker of the natures
  Of some of your great courtiers.
ANTONIO   The Lord Cardinal's,
  And other strangers, that are now in court,
  I shall.

                  [*Enter* FERDINAND]

      Here comes the great Calabrian Duke.   85
FERDINAND
  Who took the ring oft'nest?
SILVIO
  Antonio Bologna, my lord.
FERDINAND
  Our sister Duchess' great master of her household? Give
  him the jewel. When shall we leave this sportive action and
  fall to action indeed?   90
CASTRUCHIO
  Methinks, my lord, you should not desire to go to war in
  person.
FERDINAND
  Now for some gravity. Why, my lord?
CASTRUCHIO
  It is fitting a soldier arise to be a prince, but not necessary
  a prince descend to be a captain.   95

81 *presence* the ruler's audience chamber, perhaps indicated by a chair of state
  upstage
86 *took the ring* A game introduced by King James I to his court in place of jousting: the galloping horseman had to carry off the suspended ring on the point of
  his lance. NCW quote Nichols, *Progresses, Processions, and Magnificent
  Festivities of King James I*, (1828 repr. New York 1966) II, 549–50: King James'
  son Prince Charles 'mounted as it were upon a Spanish jennet that takes his
  swiftnes from the nature of the winde, most couragiously and with much agilitie
  of hand took the ring clearly four times in five courses'. Webster makes rings
  important in the play: the Duchess puts a ring on Antonio's finger at the end of
  Act I, the Cardinal takes one off her finger at III.iv.6 s.d., Ferdinand gives the
  Duchess what she takes to be Antonio's severed hand, with a ring on it, (IV.i.43),
  and the noose (see IV.ii.239) is a ring. The word also had sexual undertones
  (*Merchant of Venice*, V.i.304–7, Middleton and Rowley, *The Changeling*,
  I.ii.27–31), which are ironically implicit here.
89 *jewel* The reward for taking the ring; but again Webster may signal irony, as
  jewel could signify virginity and married chastity (as in *Cymbeline*, I.iv.153).

FERDINAND
  No?
CASTRUCHIO
  No, my lord, he were far better do it by a deputy.
FERDINAND
  Why should he not as well sleep, or eat, by a deputy? This
  might take idle, offensive, and base office from him,
  whereas the other deprives him of honour.   100
CASTRUCHIO
  Believe my experience: that <u>realm is never long in quiet
  where the ruler is a soldier.</u>
FERDINAND
  Thou told'st me thy wife could not endure fighting.
CASTRUCHIO
  True, my lord.
FERDINAND
  And of a jest she broke of a captain she met full of wounds   105
  – I have forgot it.
CASTRUCHIO
  She told him, my lord, he was a pitiful fellow to lie like the
  children of Ismael, all in tents.
FERDINAND
  Why, there's a wit were able to undo all the surgeons of the
  city: for although gallants should quarrel, and had drawn   110
  their weapons, and were ready to go to it, yet her persua-
  sions would make them put up.
CASTRUCHIO
  That she would, my lord.
[FERDINAND]
  How do you like my Spanish jennet?
RODERIGO
  He is all fire.   115

105 s.p. *FERDINAND* ed. (*Fred* Q1)
108 *children . . . tents* Arabs (See Genesis 21.9-21), tent-dwellers ; with a pun on *tent*
    meaning a dressing for a wound.
112 *put up* sheathe their weapons
114 s.p. *FERDINAND* ed. (not in Q1); in Q1 the line is inset as for all lines with a
    new speaker. It is consistent to give the line to Ferdinand in this context where
    he praises the animal and refers several more times to horses and horsemanship.
    It is unlikely that in Ferdinand's presence Castruchio would initiate a topic, and
    a *Spanish jennet* is a light sporting horse (see 86 n. above) unsuitable for an old
    lord like Castruchio.

FERDINAND

I am of Pliny's opinion, I think he was begot by the wind,
he runs as if he were ballass'd with quicksilver.

SILVIO

True, my lord, he reels from the tilt often.

RODERIGO and GRISOLAN

Ha, ha, ha!

FERDINAND

Why do you laugh? Methinks you that are courtiers should   120
be my touchwood, take fire when I give fire, that is, laugh
when I laugh, were the subject never so witty.

CASTRUCHIO

True, my lord, I myself have heard a very good jest and
have scorned to seem to have so silly a wit as to understand
it.   125

FERDINAND

But I can laugh at your fool, my lord.

CASTRUCHIO

He cannot speak, you know, but he makes faces, my lady
cannot abide him.

FERDINAND

No?

CASTRUCHIO

Nor endure to be in merry company, for she says too much   130
laughing and too much company fills her too full of the
wrinkle.

FERDINAND

I would then have a mathematical instrument made for her
face, that she might not laugh out of compass. I shall
shortly visit you at Milan, Lord Silvio.   135

SILVIO

Your grace shall arrive most welcome.

116 *Pliny's opinion* Pliny writes that Portuguese mares are said to conceive by the
   west wind (p. 222).

117 It is as if quicksilver endows the steed with added speed and liveliness – a ship
   may, like a horse, be said to *run* (as in 'run before the wind') and has ballast for
   stability; *quicksilver* suggests speed, high mobility and value, the opposite to
   cheap heavy material normally used as ballast.

118 *reels from the tilt* Quibbling on *reel* (1) swing about, be unbalanced (2) stagger
   back; and on *tilt* (1) the listing effect of uneven ballast on a ship (2) a blow in
   jousting (3) the act of copulation.

121 *when* only when

134 *out of compass* immoderately

FERDINAND

You are a good horseman, Antonio; you have excellent
riders in France: what do you think of good horsemanship?

ANTONIO

Nobly, my lord; as out of the Grecian horse issued many
famous princes, so, out of brave horsemanship arise the   140
first sparks of growing resolution that raise the mind to
noble action.

FERDINAND

You have bespoke it worthily.

[*Enter* CARDINAL, DUCHESS, CARIOLA, JULIA
and Attendants]

SILVIO

Your brother the Lord Cardinal, and sister Duchess.

CARDINAL

Are the galleys come about?   145

GRISOLAN

They are, my lord.

FERDINAND

Here's the Lord Silvio is come to take his leave.

DELIO

[*Aside to* ANTONIO] Now, sir, your promise: what's that
    Cardinal?

I mean his temper? They say he's a brave fellow,
Will play his five thousand crowns at tennis, dance,   150
Court ladies, and one that hath fought single combats.

ANTONIO

Some such flashes superficially hang on him, for form, but
observe his inward character: he is a melancholy church-
man. The spring in his face is nothing but the engend'ring
of toads. Where he is jealous of any man he lays worse plots 155
for them than ever was imposed on Hercules, for he strews
in his way flatterers, panders, intelligencers, atheists, and a
thousand such political monsters. He should have been

---

139 *Grecian horse* the proverbial Trojan horse

152 *form* outward appearance

154–5 *spring ... toads* 'his tears, in others a sign of humanity, are a slime which
breeds reptiles' – assuming *spring* means fountain: Lucas compares Chapman,
Bussy d'Ambois, 'that toadpool that stands in thy complexion'. Alternatively or
additionally, if *spring* means springtime, then in Ferdinand it generates nothing
but ugliness and poison. Webster probably remembers *Troilus and Cressida*,
II.iii.158–9: 'I do hate a proud man, as I do hate the engend'ring of toads'.

157 *flatterers* ed. (flatters Q1)
     intelligencers spies

Pope, but instead of coming to it by the primitive decency
of the Church, he did bestow bribes so largely, and so   160
impudently, as if he would have carried it away without
heaven's knowledge. Some good he hath done.

DELIO
You have given too much of him. What's his brother?

ANTONIO
The Duke there? A most perverse and turbulent nature;
What appears in him mirth is merely outside.   165
If he laugh heartily, it is to laugh
All honesty out of fashion.

DELIO   Twins?

ANTONIO   In quality.
He speaks with others' tongues, and hears men's suits
With others' ears: will seem to sleep o'th'bench
Only to entrap offenders in their answers;   170
Dooms men to death, by information,
Rewards, by hearsay.

DELIO   Then the law to him
Is like a foul black cobweb to a spider,
He makes it his dwelling, and a prison
To entangle those shall feed him.

ANTONIO   Most true: 175
He ne'er pays debts, unless they be shrewd turns,
And those he will confess that he doth owe.
Last: for his brother there, the Cardinal,
They that do flatter him most say oracles
Hang at his lips, and verily I believe them,   180
For the devil speaks in them;
But for their sister, the right noble Duchess,
You never fixed your eye on three fair medals
Cast in one figure, of so different temper.
For her discourse, it is so full of rapture   185
You only will begin then to be sorry
When she doth end her speech, and wish, in wonder,
She held it less vainglory to talk much

---

167 *In quality* In kind – but they are not actually twins, whereas it emerges in
      IV.ii.257 that Ferdinand and the Duchess are actual twins. Nevertheless Webster
      probably intended close resemblance in appearance and age between the three of
      them, as visual correlation to their psychological and emotional involvement
      with one another. This physical resemblance was stressed in RSC productions in
      1971 and 1989.

176 *shrewd* ed. (shewed Q1); *shrewd turns* injuries

183 *your* ed. (you Q1)

Than you penance, to hear her. Whilst she speaks,
She throws upon a man so sweet a look,   190
That it were able raise one to a galliard
That lay in a dead palsy, and to dote
On that sweet countenance; but in that look
There speaketh so divine a continence
As cuts off all lascivious and vain hope.   195
Her days are practised in such noble virtue
That sure her nights, nay more, her very sleeps,
Are more in heaven than other ladies' shrifts.
Let all sweet ladies break their flatt'ring glasses
And dress themselves in her.
DELIO   Fie, Antonio,   200
You play the wire-drawer with her commendations.
ANTONIO
I'll case the picture up, only thus much:
All her particular worth grows to this sum,
She stains the time past, lights the time to come.
CARIOLA
[*Aside to* ANTONIO] You must attend my lady in the gallery 205
Some half an hour hence.
ANTONIO   I shall.
FERDINAND
Sister, I have a suit to you.
DUCHESS   To me, sir?
FERDINAND
A gentleman here, Daniel de Bosola,
One that was in the galleys.
DUCHESS   Yes, I know him.

---

189 *you* ed. (your Q1) The parallel with Guazzo, *The civile conversation of M.
    Steeven Guazzo,* trans. G. Pettie (1581), (cit. Dent p. 67), indicates that Q1's
    your is an error: the Cardinal's devilishness is contrasted to the Duchess' reli-
    gious virtue. In Guazzo, although the Duchess' discourses are said to be 'delight-
    ful' and her smile 'sweet' enough to attract men, her 'continency' leads men to
    religious virtue.
    Than you penance Than you hold it spiritually purifying
191 *galliard* a lively dance
198 *shrifts* confessions
199 *glasses* looking-glasses, mirrors
200 *dress ... her* (1) use her as a mirror (2) adopt her virtues as their own
201 *play the wire-drawer* spin out to an excessive degree
202 *case the picture up* put the picture away in its case
204 *stains* eclipses, puts into the shade

FERDINAND
  A worthy fellow h'is. Pray let me entreat for   210
  The provisorship of your horse.
DUCHESS   Your knowledge of him
  Commends him, and prefers him.
FERDINAND   Call him hither.

                              [Exit ATTENDANT]

  We are now upon parting. Good Lord Silvio,
  Do us commend to all our noble friends
  At the leaguer.
SILVIO   Sir, I shall.
[DUCHESS]   You are for Milan?
SILVIO   I am.   215
DUCHESS
  Bring the caroches – we'll bring you down to the haven.

        [Exeunt ALL *but* FERDINAND *and the* CARDINAL]

CARDINAL
  Be sure you entertain that Bosola
  For your intelligence; I would not be seen in't,
  <u>And therefore many times I have slighted him,</u>
  When he did court our furtherance – as this morning.   220
FERDINAND
  Antonio, the great master of her household,
  Had been far fitter.
CARDINAL   You are deceived in him,
  <u>His nature is too honest for such business.</u>

               [Enter BOSOLA]

  He comes. I'll leave you.   *[Exit]*
BOSOLA   I was lured to you.

211 *provisorship of your horse* An important and valuable court appointment:
    Queen Elizabeth I gave the equivalent post in her court to her favourite, Robert
    Dudley, later Earl of Leicester.
213 *are* ed. (not in Q1)
215 *leaguer* ed. (leagues Q1); = military camp, especially one engaged in a siege
215 s.p. *DUCHESS* ed. (*Ferd* Q1). Attribution of the speech in Q1 to Ferdinand
    cannot be right since he already knows Silvio's destination (see his preceding
    speech and line 135). If the Duchess speaks this line then her next speech at line
    216 is prepared for.
216 *caroches* elegant coaches
217–8 *entertain ... intelligence* keep that Bosola on your payroll as your secret agent
220 *court ... furtherance* ask us for reward

FERDINAND
My brother here, the Cardinal, could never   225
Abide you.
BOSOLA   Never since he was in my debt.
FERDINAND
May be some oblique character in your face
Made him suspect you?
BOSOLA   Doth he study physiognomy?
There's no more credit to be given to th'face
Than to a sick man's urine, which some call   230
The physician's whore, because she cozens him.
He did suspect me wrongfully.
FERDINAND   For that
You must give great men leave to take their times:
Distrust doth cause us seldom be deceived;
You see, the oft shaking of the cedar tree   235
Fastens it more at root.
BOSOLA   Yet take heed:
For to suspect a friend unworthily
Instructs him the next way to suspect you,
And prompts him to deceive you.
[FERDINAND]   There's gold.
BOSOLA   So:
What follows? Never rained such showers as these   240
Without thunderbolts i'th'tail of them.
Whose throat must I cut?
FERDINAND
Your inclination to shed blood rides post
Before my occasion to use you. I give you that
To live i'th'court here and observe the Duchess,   245
To note all the particulars of her haviour:
What suitors do solicit her for marriage
And whom she best affects. She's a young widow,
I would not have her marry again.
BOSOLA   No, sir?
FERDINAND
Do not you ask the reason, but be satisfied   250
I say I would not.

---

231 *cozens* deceives
238 *next* nearest
239 s.p. ed. (*Berd* Q1)
240–1 *rained . . . tail* Alluding to the shower of gold, in which form Jupiter visited
     Danae.
241–2 ed. (one line Q1)
243 *rides post* runs ahead

BOSOLA   It seems you would create me
  One of your familiars.
FERDINAND   Familiar? What's that?
BOSOLA
  Why, a very quaint invisible devil in flesh:
  An intelligencer.
FERDINAND   Such a kind of thriving thing
  I would wish thee: and ere long thou mayst arrive   255
  At a higher place by't.
BOSOLA   Take your devils,
  Which hell calls angels: these cursed gifts would make
  You a corrupter, me an impudent traitor,
  And should I take these they'd take me to hell.
FERDINAND
  Sir, I'll take nothing from you that I have given.   260
  There is a place that I procured for you
  This morning, the provisorship o'th'horse.
  Have you heard on't?
BOSOLA   No.
FERDINAND   'Tis yours: is't not worth thanks?
BOSOLA
  I would have you curse yourself now, that your bounty,
  Which makes men truly noble, e'er should make   265
  Me a villain: oh, that to avoid ingratitude
  For the good deed you have done me, I must do
  All the ill man can invent. Thus the devil
  Candies all sins o'er: and what heaven terms vile,
  That names he complemental.
FERDINAND   Be yourself: 270
  Keep your old garb of melancholy, 'twill express
  You envy those that stand above your reach,
  Yet strive not to come near 'em. This will gain

252 *familiars* Quibbling on the senses (1) members of the household (2) familiar spirits (3) intimate friends – presumably Ferdinand's reaction is to (3), on snobbish grounds, he being at this point unmoved by the implications of (2): on which see below 304 n.

253 *quaint* cunning

257 *angels* The gold coins called nobles, familiarly known as angels, bore the image of St Michael killing a dragon. The same pun appears in *The Revenger's Tragedy*, II.i.88: 'forty angels can make four score devils'.

259 *to* ed. (not in Q1)

263 *on't* ed. (out Q1)

269 *o'er* ed. (are Q1)

270 *complemental* polite accomplishment

Access to private lodgings, where yourself
May, like a politic dormouse –
BOSOLA   As I have seen some   275
Feed in a lord's dish, half asleep, not seeming
To listen to any talk, and yet these rogues
Have cut his throat in a dream. What's my place?
The provisorship o'th'horse? Say then my corruption
Grew out of horse dung. I am your creature.   280
FERDINAND
Away!
BOSOLA
Let good men, for good deeds, covet good fame,
Since place and riches oft are bribes of shame.
Sometimes the devil doth preach.   *Exit*

[*Enter* CARDINAL *and* DUCHESS]

CARDINAL
We are to part from you, and your own discretion   285
Must now be your director.
FERDINAND   You are a widow:
You know already what man is, and therefore
Let not youth, high promotion, eloquence –
CARDINAL
No, nor any thing without the addition, honour,
Sway your high blood.
FERDINAND   Marry? They are most luxurious   290
Will wed twice.
CARDINAL   O fie!
FERDINAND   Their livers are more spotted
Than Laban's sheep.

275 *politic* cunning
      dormouse According to Pliny (p. 233) the dormouse renews its strength and
      youth by sleeping all the winter.
276 *Feed ... dish* Dine at a lord's table. See *The Malcontent*, II.iii.42–4: 'Lay one into
      his breast shall sleep with him, / Feed in the same dish, run in self faction, / Who
      may discover any shape of danger'.
279 *provisorship* ed. (Prouisors-ship Q1)
284 Proverbial – Tilley D230 and D266.
285–6 *your ... director* you must rely on your own judgement
290 *high blood* (1) noble lineage (2) passionate nature
      luxurious lecherous
291 *livers* The organ was associated with passions, from lust to love: see *As You Like
      It,* III.ii.422–4.
292 *Laban's sheep* See Genesis 30.31–43; but the phrase probably comes from
      Whetstone, *Heptameron* (1582): 'a company as spotted as *Labans* Sheepe' (Dent).

DUCHESS   Diamonds are of most value
  They say, that have passed through most jewellers' hands.
FERDINAND
  Whores, by that rule, are precious.
DUCHESS   Will you hear me?
  I'll never marry.
CARDINAL   So most widows say,   295
  But commonly that motion lasts no longer
  Than the turning of an hourglass: the funeral sermon,
  And it, end both together.
FERDINAND   Now hear me:
  You live in a rank pasture here, i'th'court.
  There is a kind of honey-dew that's deadly: 300
  'Twill poison your fame. Look to't. Be not cunning:
  For they whose faces do belie their hearts
  Are witches ere they arrive at twenty years,
  Ay, and give the devil suck.
DUCHESS
  This is terrible good counsel.   305
FERDINAND
  Hypocrisy is woven of a fine small thread
  Subtler than Vulcan's engine: yet, believe't,
  Your darkest actions, nay, your privat'st thoughts,
  Will come to light.
CARDINAL   You may flatter yourself
  And take your own choice: privately be married   310
  Under the eves of night.
FERDINAND   Think't the best voyage
  That e'er you made, like the irregular crab
  Which, though't goes backward, thinks that it goes right
  Because it goes its own way; but observe:

295 *marry.* ed. (marry: Q1) I assume Q1's colon after *marry* signifies a full-stop, as
    frequently with Crane: but if the colon is interpreted as indicating interruption,
    (so the 1980 Royal Exchange production, and NCW) the Duchess is not guilty
    of deliberate deception here.
296 *motion* impulse
300 *honey-dew* sweet sticky substance found on plants, formerly supposed a kind of
    dew. In *The Malcontent*, III.ii.27–50, Malevole memorably evokes the luxury of
    an Italian court: 'The strongest incitements to immodesty – / To have her bound,
    incensed with wanton sweets, / Her veins filled high with heating delicates ...'
304 Witches supposedly suckled familiar spirits, usually animals, from an extra
    nipple.
307 *Vulcan's engine* Vulcan used a net of very fine thread to catch Venus and Mars
    in adultery.

Such weddings may more properly be said   315
To be executed than celebrated.
CARDINAL   The marriage night
Is the entrance into some prison.
FERDINAND   And those joys,
Those lustful pleasures, are like heavy sleeps
Which do forerun man's mischief.
CARDINAL   Fare you well.
Wisdom begins at the end: remember it.   [*Exit*]   320
DUCHESS
I think this speech between you both was studied,
It came so roundly off.
FERDINAND   You are my sister.
This was my father's poniard: do you see?
I'd be loath to see't look rusty, 'cause 'twas his.
I would have you to give o'er these chargeable revels;   325
A visor and a masque are whispering rooms
That were ne'er built for goodness. Fare ye well –
And women like that part which, like the lamprey,
Hath ne'er a bone in't.
DUCHESS   Fie sir!
FERDINAND   Nay,
I mean the tongue: variety of courtship.   330

316 Both these verbs could be used equally of religious rites, but Ferdinand implies
the alternative meaning of *executed* = put to death.
320 Alluding to the proverbs 'Think on the end before you begin' (Tilley E125) and
'Remember the end' (E128).
321 *studied* prepared in advance, rehearsed. If the brothers take positions on either
side of the Duchess the episode's general parallels with *The Revenger's Tragedy*,
IV.iv (the interrogation by Vindice and Hippolito, with daggers drawn, of their
mother) are apparent; at the same time in Webster each brother is driven by a
different obsession: Ferdinand's is sexual, the Cardinal's is social rank. See also
II.v below.
323–4 *poniard ... rusty* If he uses the dagger to kill her, its tempered steel will be
bloody and start to rust: see Juliet's last words, in *Romeo and Juliet*, V.iii.170.
Vindice in *The Revenger's Tragedy*, IV.iv.43–5, sheathing his dagger when his
mother begins to weep, says 'Brother it rains, 'twill spoil your dagger, house it'.
325 *chargeable revels* expensive court festivities. The elaborate masques at the court
of James I were notoriously expensive.
326–7 In *The Revenger's Tragedy*, I.iv.27ff., Antonio describes a court masque 'last
revelling night' where 'torchlight made an artificial noon' and a murderer wore
a mask as disguise; and Spurio tells (I.ii.185–6) of a court feast and 'a whispering and withdrawing hour / When base male bawds kept sentinel at stair-head'.
328 *lamprey* an eel-like fish

What cannot a neat knave with a smooth tale
Make a woman believe? Farewell, lusty widow.   [*Exit*]
DUCHESS
Shall this move me? If all my royal kindred
Lay in my way unto this marriage
I'd make them my low foot-steps, and even now,   335
Even in this hate, as men in some great battles,
By apprehending danger have achieved
Almost impossible actions – I have heard soldiers say so –
So I, through frights and threat'nings will assay
This dangerous venture. Let old wives report   340
I winked and chose a husband.

                    [*Enter* CARIOLA]

                        Cariola,
To thy known secrecy I have given up
More than my life, my fame.
CARIOLA   Both shall be safe:
For I'll conceal this secret from the world
As warily as those that trade in poison   345
Keep poison from their children.
DUCHESS   Thy protestation
Is ingenious and hearty: I believe it.
Is Antonio come?
CARIOLA   He attends you.
DUCHESS   Good dear soul.
Leave me: but place thyself behind the arras,
Where thou mayst overhear us. Wish me good speed,   350
For I am going into a wilderness
Where I shall find nor path, nor friendly clew
To be my guide.

331 *tale* Punning on the sense 'penis' (see *Romeo and Juliet,* II.iv.97).

335 *foot-steps* steps (up to the altar)

341 *winked* closed my eyes. The proverb 'You may wink and choose' (Tilley W501)
    meant 'choose blind' – but *wink* also meant 'shut your eyes at wrong', in which
    case the Duchess anticipates moral condemnation and dismisses it as no better
    than the prejudice of old wives.

343 s.p. ed. (*Carolia* Q1)

343 *fame* reputation

347 *ingenious and hearty* sagacious and heartfelt

349 *arras* curtain – hung across the back of the stage (later, in IV.i, a curtain is drawn
    to display the figures of Antonio and the children)

350 *Where ... us* The staging recalls two episodes involving Polonius in *Hamlet,*
    III.i.54ff. and III.iv.6ff.

352 *clew* ball of thread used as a guide (as by Theseus to guide him through the labyrinth)

[CARIOLA *withdraws behind the arras*]

[*Enter* ANTONIO]

          I sent for you. Sit down:
  Take pen and ink and write. Are you ready?
ANTONIO   Yes.
DUCHESS
  What did I say?
ANTONIO   That I should write somewhat.   355
DUCHESS
  Oh, I remember:
  After these triumphs and this large expense
  It's fit – like thrifty husbands – we enquire
  What's laid up for tomorrow.
ANTONIO
  So please your beauteous excellence.
DUCHESS   Beauteous?   360
  Indeed I thank you: I look young for your sake.
  You have ta'en my cares upon you.
ANTONIO [*Rising*]   I'll fetch your grace
  The particulars of your revenue and expense.
DUCHESS
  Oh, you are an upright treasurer: but you mistook,
  For when I said I meant to make enquiry   365
  What's laid up for tomorrow, I did mean
  What's laid up yonder for me.
ANTONIO   Where?
DUCHESS   In heaven.
  I am making my will, as 'tis fit princes should
  In perfect memory, and I pray sir, tell me
  Were not one better make it smiling, thus,   370
  Than in deep groans and terrible ghastly looks,

---

357 *these* ed. (this Q1)
     triumphs court festivities
358 *thrifty husbands* provident managers (of the court and ducal household) – but
    the Duchess lightly hints at *husband* = marriage partner, the sense in 399
359 *laid up* in store
360–1 ed. (one line Q1)
361 *for your sake* thanks to you – and with the hinted sense 'for love of you'
362–3 ed. (... Grace the / Particulars ... Q1)
364 *upright* Punning on the fact that Antonio has just stood up (NCW).
366 See Matthew 6 particularly 19–21: 'lay up for yourselves treasure in heaven ...
    for where your treasure is there will your heart be also' – but the whole chapter
    is highly relevant.

As if the gifts we parted with procured
That violent distraction?
ANTONIO   Oh, much better.
DUCHESS
  If I had a husband now, this care were quit:
  But I intend to make you overseer.   375
  What good deed shall we first remember? Say.
ANTONIO
  Begin with that first good deed began i'th'world
  After man's creation, the sacrament of marriage.
  I'd have you first provide for a good husband,
  Give him all.
DUCHESS   All?
ANTONIO   Yes, your excellent self.   380
DUCHESS
  In a winding sheet?
ANTONIO   In a couple.
DUCHESS
  St Winifred, that were a strange will!
ANTONIO
  'Twere strange if there were no will in you
  To marry again.
DUCHESS   What do you think of marriage?
ANTONIO
  I take't as those that deny purgatory: 385
  It locally contains or heaven or hell;
  There's no third place in't.
DUCHESS   How do you affect it?

372 *procured* were the cause of
373 *distraction* Q3 (distruction Q1)
375 *overseer* person appointed under the terms of a will to supervise or assist its
     executors
381 *winding sheet* So making her fit to accompany her dead husband. There was
     apparently a fashion for women to be buried in their wedding sheets – see Clare
     Gittings, *Death, Burial, and the Individual in Early Modern England* (1984), pp.
     111–12.
382 *Winifred.* ed. (*Winfrid* Q1); Q1 is an error since St Winfred – Wynfrith – was
     then universally known as St Boniface. *St Winifred*, a Welsh saint of the 7th cen-
     tury whose head, struck off by Caradoc ap Alauc for refusing his love, was
     restored to life by St Beuno, is invoked by the Duchess because she sees an apt
     parallel with her own situation.
385–7 Protestants denied the existence of purgatory; some proverbs averred that
     marriage was heaven or hell, others that it was purgatory or hell (Dent).
387 *affect* like, feel about

ANTONIO
  My banishment, feeding my melancholy,
  Would often reason thus –
DUCHESS   Pray let's hear it.
ANTONIO
  Say a man never marry, nor have children,   390
  What takes that from him? Only the bare name
  Of being a father, or the weak delight
  To see the little wanton ride a-cock-horse
  Upon a painted stick, or hear him chatter
  Like a taught starling.
DUCHESS   Fie, fie, what's all this?   395
  One of your eyes is blood-shot, use my ring to't,
              [*Gives him the ring*]
  They say 'tis very sovereign: 'twas my wedding ring,
  And I did vow never to part with it
  But to my second husband.
ANTONIO
  You have parted with it now.   400
DUCHESS
  Yes, to help your eyesight.
ANTONIO
  You have made me stark blind.
DUCHESS
  How?
ANTONIO
  There is a saucy and ambitious devil
  Is dancing in this circle.
DUCHESS   Remove him.
ANTONIO   How?   405
DUCHESS
  There needs small conjuration when your finger
  May do it: thus –
        [*She puts her ring upon his finger*]
      – is it fit?
        He kneels
ANTONIO   What said you?
DUCHESS   Sir,
  This goodly roof of yours is too low built,
  I cannot stand upright in't, nor discourse,
  Without I raise it higher. Raise yourself,   410
  Or if you please, my hand to help you: so.

388 *banishment* When he accompanied Federico to France (see above 2 n.).
393 *wanton* rogue
397 *sovereign* efficacious: so gold is believed to cure a stye on an eyelid

[He rises]

ANTONIO
Ambition, madam, is a great man's madness,
That is not kept in chains and close-pent rooms
But in fair lightsome lodgings, and is girt
With the wild noise of prattling visitants   415
Which makes it lunatic beyond all cure.
Conceive not I am so stupid but I aim
Whereto your favours tend: but he's a fool
That being a-cold would thrust his hands i'th'fire
To warm them.
DUCHESS   So now the ground's broke   420
You may discover what a wealthy mine
I make you lord of.
ANTONIO   Oh my unworthiness.
DUCHESS
You were ill to sell yourself.
This dark'ning of your worth is not like that
Which tradesmen use i'th'city: their false lights   425
Are to rid bad wares off; and I must tell you,
If you will know where breathes a complete man –
I speak it without flattery – turn your eyes
And progress through yourself.
ANTONIO
Were there nor heaven nor hell   430
I should be honest: I have long served virtue
And ne'er ta'en wages of her.
DUCHESS   Now she pays it.
The misery of us that are born great,
We are forced to woo because none dare woo us:
And as a tyrant doubles with his words,   435
And fearfully equivocates, so we
Are forced to express our violent passions
In riddles and in dreams, and leave the path
Of simple virtue which was never made
To seem the thing it is not. Go, go brag   440
You have left me heartless, mine is in your bosom,
I hope 'twill multiply love there. You do tremble.
Make not your heart so dead a piece of flesh
To fear more than to love me. Sir, be confident,
What is't distracts you? This is flesh and blood, sir, 445

---

417 *aim* guess
422 *of* ed. (off Q1)
426 *rid ... off* get rid of bad wares
445 *flesh and blood* Proverbial: 'To be flesh and blood as others are' (Tilley F367).

'Tis not the figure cut in alabaster
Kneels at my husband's tomb. Awake, awake, man,
I do here put off all vain ceremony
And only do appear to you a young widow
That claims you for her husband; and like a widow,   450
I use but half a blush in't.
ANTONIO   Truth speak for me,
I will remain the constant sanctuary
Of your good name.
DUCHESS   I thank you, gentle love,
And 'cause you shall not come to me in debt,
Being now my steward, here upon your lips   455
I sign your *Quietus est.*
                    [*She kisses him*]
This you should have begged now.
I have seen children oft eat sweet-meats thus
As fearful to devour them too soon.
ANTONIO
But for your brothers?
DUCHESS   Do not think of them.   460
                    [*Embraces him*]
All discord, without this circumference,
Is only to be pitied and not feared.
Yet, should they know it, time will easily
Scatter the tempest.
ANTONIO   These words should be mine,
And all the parts you have spoke, if some part of it   465
Would not have savoured flattery.
DUCHESS   Kneel.

          [CARIOLA *comes from behind the arras*]

ANTONIO   Ha?

446-7 *figure ... tomb* For this comparison see *Merchant of Venice*, I.i.83–4. It is a
    further unwittingly ironic anticipation of tragedy: the Duchess has referred to her
    will and winding-sheet, Antonio to imprisonment and the visits of madmen; even
    a cold hand will recur – see IV.i.50. Elizabethan sculptures were usually poly-
    chrome and realistic; in a play an actor could represent a stone figure, as in *The
    Winter's Tale*, V.iii, or a waxwork, as in IV.i.54 below.

456 *Quietus est* Latin: 'he is discharged of payment due' – a conventional phrase
    indicating that accounts are correct; but with an ominous undertone: it could
    also refer to release from one's debt to nature, death, as in *Hamlet*, III.i.74.

461 *without this circumference* outside my arms' embrace (also perhaps referring to
    the ring)

465 *parts* particulars

DUCHESS
Be not amazed, this woman's of my counsel.
I have heard lawyers say a contract in a chamber,
Per verba de presenti, is absolute marriage:
Bless, heaven, this sacred Gordian, which let violence   470
Never untwine.
ANTONIO   And may our sweet affections, like the spheres,
Be still in motion –
DUCHESS   Quick'ning, and make
The like soft music –
ANTONIO   That we may imitate the loving palms,
Best emblem of a peaceful marriage,
That ne'er bore fruit divided.   475
DUCHESS
What can the Church force more?
ANTONIO
That Fortune may not know an accident
Either of joy, or sorrow, to divide
Our fixed wishes.
DUCHESS   How can the Church build faster?
We now are man and wife, and 'tis the Church   480
That must but echo this. Maid, stand apart,
I now am blind.
ANTONIO   What's your conceit in this?
DUCHESS
I would have you lead your Fortune by the hand
Unto your marriage bed.
You speak in me this, for we now are one.   485

---

469 *Per ... presenti* A term in canon law, 'by words, as from the present': the
Elizabethan church recognised as a marriage the simple declaration by a couple
that they were man and wife, even without a witness. See *Measure for Measure*,
I.ii.145ff.: 'Upon a true contract ...'; *de* ed. (not in Q1).

470–1 *Bless ... untwine* The Duchess refers to her hand clasping Antonio's.

470 *Gordian* The oracle decreed that anyone who could loose the knot tied by King
Gordius would rule Asia. Alexander the Great had to cut it with his sword.

471–3 The planetary spheres supposedly created music by their perpetual (*still*), stim-
ulating (*Quick'ning*) and unheard (*soft*) harmonious motion.

476 *force* enforce

479 *build* Q1 (bind Brown); Some editors conjecture that 'bind' stood in Crane's
copy but that in transcribing he erroneously used too many minim strokes; these
the compositor interpreted as 'uil': but this is unconvincing – why add a letter 'l'
which is not a minim? Q1 makes sense (a marriage needs to be firmly built) and
should stand, even though as some editors argue, 'bind' better relates to the pass-
age's concern with tying together.
faster more strongly and firmly

We'll only lie, and talk, together, and plot
T'appease my humorous kindred; and if you please,
Like the old tale in Alexander and Lodowick,
Lay a naked sword between us, keep us chaste.
Oh, let me shroud my blushes in your bosom,   490
Since 'tis the treasury of all my secrets.

> [*Exeunt* DUCHESS *and* ANTONIO]

CARIOLA
Whether the spirit of greatness or of woman
Reign most in her, I know not, but it shows
A fearful madness. I owe her much of pity.   *Exit*

Act II, Scene i

> [*Enter* BOSOLA *and* CASTRUCHIO]

BOSOLA
You say you would fain be taken for an eminent courtier?
CASTRUCHIO
'Tis the very main of my ambition.
BOSOLA
Let me see: you have a reasonable good face for't already,
and your night-cap expresses your ears sufficient largely. I

---

487 *humorous* ill-humoured, difficult
488 An extant ballad tells how the two friends were so alike they were mistaken for
     each other. When Lodowick married a princess in Alexander's name, he laid a
     naked sword each night between himself and the princess, because he would not
     wrong his friend.
490 *shroud* hide from view; but the verb also had the ominous sense 'prepare for
     burial' (*OED* v7)
492–4 Cariola remains on stage alone, which gives added force to her anxious asser-
     tion that her mistress is showing a *fearful madness*.

  0 s.d. ed. (ACTUS II. SCENA I. / *Bosola, Castruchio, an Old Lady, Antonio,
     Delio, Duchesse, Rodorico, Grisolan.* Q1)
  1–44 ed. (as verse Q1)
  1 *courtier* lawyer, judge, identified by the white coif or skull-cap (see line 4 below,
     your night-cap) worn by a sergeant-at-law. The usual sense of *courtier* may also
     apply, as senior lawyers might well attend the ruler's court.
  2 *main* purpose
  4 *expresses … largely* shows off your long ears (and makes you look a complete
     ass)

would have you learn to twirl the strings of your band with   5
a good grace; and in a set speech, at th'end of every
sentence, to hum three or four times, or blow your nose till
it smart again, to recover your memory. When you come to
be a president in criminal causes, if you smile upon a
prisoner, hang him, but if you frown upon him, and   10
threaten him, let him be sure to 'scape the gallows.

CASTRUCHIO
I would be a very merry president.

BOSOLA
Do not sup a-nights, 'twill beget you an admirable wit.

CASTRUCHIO
Rather it would make me have a good stomach to quarrel,
for they say your roaring boys eat meat seldom, and that   15
makes them so valiant. But how shall I know whether the
people take me for an eminent fellow?

BOSOLA
I will teach a trick to know it: give out you lie a-dying, and
if you hear the common people curse you, be sure you are
taken for one of the prime night-caps.   20

[*Enter* OLD LADY]

You come from painting now?

OLD LADY
From what?

BOSOLA
Why, from your scurvy face physic. To behold thee not
painted inclines somewhat near a miracle. These in thy face,
here, were deep ruts and foul sloughs the last progress.   25
There was a lady in France that, having had the smallpox,
flayed the skin off her face to make it more level; and
whereas before she looked like a nutmeg grater, after she
resembled an abortive hedgehog.

OLD LADY
Do you call this painting?   30

BOSOLA
No, no, but careening of an old morphewed lady, to make

---

5 *twirl ... band* Said to be a fashionable habit of courtiers and lawyers – Brown
   cites Jonson, *Cynthia's Revels*, V.iv.158.
15 *roaring boys* rowdies, yobs, louts
25 *sloughs* muddy holes in the road
    progress ceremonious royal journey
31 *but* ed. (but you call Q1; but you call it Q3; but I call it *Lucas*)
    careening ... lady giving an old lady's leprous hull a good scraping

her disembogue again. There's rough cast phrase to your
plastic.

OLD LADY

It seems you are well acquainted with my closet?

BOSOLA

One would suspect it for a shop of witchcraft, to find in it   35
the fat of serpents, spawn of snakes, Jews' spittle, and their
young children's ordures, and all these for the face: I would
sooner eat a dead pigeon, taken from the soles of the feet of
one sick of the plague, than kiss one of you fasting. Here
are two of you whose sin of your youth is the very patri-   40
mony of the physician, makes him renew his foot-cloth
with the spring, and change his high-priced courtesan with
the fall of the leaf. I do wonder you do not loathe yourselves.

Observe my meditation now.   45

What thing is in this outward form of man
To be beloved? We account it ominous
If nature do produce a colt, or lamb,
A fawn, or goat, in any limb resembling
A man; and fly from't as a prodigy.   50
Man stands amazed to see his deformity
In any other creature but himself;
But in our own flesh, though we bear diseases
Which have their true names only ta'en from beasts –

---

32 *disembogue* put out to sea, on the war-path

32–3 *There's ... plastic* That's coarsely put – rough-cast (lime and gravel) crude
plaster, not your smooth finish.

37 *children's* ed. (children Q1)

38–9 *dead ... plague* In 1612 when the heir to the English throne Prince Henry
lay mortally ill, freshly killed pigeons were applied to the soles of his feet. The
same treatment is recommended (for the plague) in *The English Huswife*
(1615).

39 *kiss ... fasting* Fasting supposedly makes bad breath even worse.

41 *foot-cloth* a rich cloth laid over the horse's back and hanging down to the
ground, protecting the rider from dirt: a mark of high status

42 *high-priced* She is, like the foot-cloth, an expensive status-symbol.

45–61 See *Measure for Measure*, III.i.5ff., where the Duke-as-Friar delivers to
young Claudio similar advocacy: 'Be absolute for death'. The difference here is
that instead of a young man there is an old lord and old lady. In performance, if
Bosola addresses them directly his words will seem calculatedly cruel, but if he
stands apart and addresses the audience, the two old people will serve as visible
instances of man's *deformity*.

As the most ulcerous wolf, and swinish measle –   55
Though we are eaten up of lice, and worms,
And though continually we bear about us
A rotten and dead body, we delight
To hide it in rich tissue; all our fear –
Nay all our terror – is, lest our physician   60
Should put us in the ground, to be made sweet.
[*To* CASTRUCHIO] Your wife's gone to Rome: you two couple,
and get you to the wells at Lucca, to recover your aches.

        [*Exeunt* CASTRUCHIO *and* OLD LADY]

I have other work on foot. I observe our Duchess
Is sick a-days, she pukes, her stomach seethes,   65
The fins of her eyelids look most teeming blue,
She wanes i'th'cheek, and waxes fat i'th'flank;
And contrary to our Italian fashion
Wears a loose-bodied gown. There's somewhat in't.
I have a trick may chance discover it,   70
A pretty one: I have bought some apricots,
The first our spring yields.

      [*Enter* ANTONIO *and* DELIO *talking apart*]

DELIO   And so long since married?
  You amaze me.
ANTONIO   Let me seal your lips for ever,
For did I think that anything but th'air
Could carry these words from you, I should wish   75
You had no breath at all.
[*To* BOSOLA] Now sir, in your contemplation? You are
studying to become a great wise fellow?

---

55 *ulcerous wolf* In Latin *lupus* means ulcer, and *wolf* was the Elizabethan name for
  a type of ulcer.
  measle The disease of measles in humans, also a disease in swine: both diseases
  etymologically confused with *mesel* = leprous (*OED*).
59 *tissue* delicate cloth
61 *sweet* benign in effect
62–3 ed. (as verse Q1)
63 *wells at Lucca* The Italian city was famous as a spa.
  recover your aches The waters are to alleviate the symptoms of venereal disease
  (commonly called 'the bone-ache').
66 The edges of her eyelids are blue, like those of a pregnant woman (Lucas).
68–9 *contrary … gown* Bosola, having listed physical signs associated with pregnancy, then observes the Duchess' unusual choice of gown, which could conceal
  the most obvious sign; there is an innuendo in *loose-bodied* = morally loose.

BOSOLA

Oh sir, the opinion of wisdom is a foul tetter that runs all over a man's body: if simplicity direct us to have no evil, it   80
directs us to a happy being. For the subtlest folly proceeds from the subtlest wisdom. Let me be simply honest.

ANTONIO

I do understand your inside.

BOSOLA

Do you so?

ANTONIO

Because you would not seem to appear to th'world puffed   85
up with your preferment, you continue this out-of-fashion melancholy; leave it, leave it.

BOSOLA

Give me leave to be honest in any phrase, in any compliment whatsoever. Shall I confess myself to you? I look no higher than I can reach: they are the gods that must ride on   90
winged horses, a lawyer's mule of a slow pace will both suit my disposition and business, for, mark me, when a man's mind rides faster than his horse can gallop, they quickly both tire.

ANTONIO

You would look up to heaven, but I think the devil that   95
rules i'th'air stands in your light.

BOSOLA

Oh, sir, you are lord of the ascendant, chief man with the Duchess, a duke was your cousin-german, removed. Say you were lineally descended from King Pippin, or he himself, what of this? Search the heads of the greatest rivers in   100
the world, you shall find them but bubbles of water. Some would think the souls of princes were brought forth by some more weighty cause than those of meaner persons; they are deceived, there's the same hand to them, the like passions sway them; the same reason that makes a vicar go   105

---

79 *tetter* skin eruption

83–123 ed. (as verse Q1)

95–6 *devil . . . air* So referred to in the Bishop's Bible, Ephesians 2.2: he 'that ruleth in the ayre'.

97 *lord . . . ascendant* the dominant influence, the rising star. In astrology the *lord* is the planet of which the associated zodiac sign is at the moment *the ascendant* – is entering the 'first house', that part of the sky which is rising above the horizon.

98 *cousin-german, removed* first cousin, once removed

99 *King Pippin* Died 768: King of the Franks and father of Charlemagne.

101–8 Derived from Montaigne, *Essayes*, II.xii, p. 274.

to law for a tithe-pig, and undo his neighbours, makes them
spoil a whole province, and batter down goodly cities with
the cannon.

[*Enter* DUCHESS *with* ATTENDANTS]

DUCHESS

Your arm, Antonio. Do I not grow fat? I am exceeding
short-winded. Bosola, I would have you, sir, provide for me   110
a litter, such a one as the Duchess of Florence rode in.

BOSOLA

The Duchess used one when she was great with child.

DUCHESS

I think she did. [*To an Attendant*] Come hither, mend my
ruff, here, when? Thou art such a tedious lady, and thy
breath smells of lemon peels, would thou hadst done; shall   115
I swoon under thy fingers? I am so troubled with the
mother.

BOSOLA

[*Aside*] I fear too much.

DUCHESS

[*To* ANTONIO] I have heard you say that the French
courtiers wear their hats on 'fore the King.   120

ANTONIO

I have seen it.

DUCHESS

In the presence?

ANTONIO

Yes.

[DUCHESS]

Why should not we bring up that fashion?
'Tis ceremony more than duty that consists   125
In the removing of a piece of felt.
Be you the example to the rest o'th'court,
Put on your hat first.

ANTONIO   You must pardon me:
I have seen, in colder countries than in France,
Nobles stand bare to th'prince; and the distinction   130
Methought showed reverently.

---

109 *fat* An attempt to explain away her advanced state of pregnancy.
117 *the mother* hysteria
118 *too* ed. (to Q1)
120 *courtiers* ed. (courties Q1)
124 s.p. ed. (not in Q1, but added by hand in many copies)
131 *Methought* ed. (My thought Q1)

BOSOLA
  I have a present for your grace.
DUCHESS   For me sir?
BOSOLA
  Apricots, madam.
DUCHESS   Oh sir, where are they?
  I have heard of none to-year.
BOSOLA [*Aside*]   Good, her colour rises.
DUCHESS
  Indeed I thank you, they are wondrous fair ones.   135
  What an unskilful fellow is our gardener,
  We shall have none this month.
BOSOLA
  Will not your grace pare them?
DUCHESS
  No – they taste of musk, methinks, indeed they do.
BOSOLA
  I know not: yet I wish your grace had pared 'em.   140
DUCHESS
  Why?
BOSOLA I forgot to tell you, the knave gardener,
  Only to raise his profit by them the sooner,
  Did ripen them in horse dung.
DUCHESS   Oh you jest.
  You shall judge: pray taste one.
ANTONIO   Indeed madam,
  I do not love the fruit.
DUCHESS   Sir, you are loath   145
  To rob us of our dainties: 'tis a delicate fruit,
  They say they are restorative?
BOSOLA
  'Tis a pretty art, this grafting.
DUCHESS
  'Tis so: a bett'ring of nature.
BOSOLA
  To make a pippin grow upon a crab,   150

---

146 *dainties* (1) choice foods (2) luxuries – with a sexual innuendo
148 *grafting* Ironically alluding to the union of the Duchess with someone of inferior
    stock (see *The Winter's Tale*, IV.iv.86ff.); this verb also had an indecent sense,
    played upon here.
150–1 An instance of Webster's detailed use of sources, here Breton, *Wil of Wit*
    (1606) Iir: 'Is not the Damson tree ... aboue the Blackthorne tree? is not the
    Pippin ... aboue the crabtree? the Abricock above the common plum?' (cited by
    Dent).

A damson on a blackthorn. [*Aside*] – How greedily she eats
  them!
A whirlwind strike off these bawd farthingales!
For, but for that, and the loose-bodied gown,
I should have discovered apparently
The young springal cutting a caper in her belly.   155
DUCHESS
I thank you, Bosola, they were right good ones,
If they do not make me sick.
ANTONIO   How now madam?
DUCHESS
This green fruit and my stomach are not friends.
How they swell me!
BOSOLA [*Aside*]   Nay, you are too much swelled already.
DUCHESS
Oh, I am in an extreme cold sweat.
BOSOLA   I am very sorry.   160
DUCHESS
Lights to my chamber. Oh, good Antonio,
I fear I am undone.   *Exit*
DELIO   Lights there, lights.

                [*Exeunt all but* ANTONIO *and* DELIO]

ANTONIO
O my most trusty Delio, we are lost.
I fear she's fall'n in labour, and there's left
No time for her remove.
DELIO   Have you prepared   165
Those ladies to attend her, and procured
That politic safe conveyance for the midwife
Your Duchess plotted?
ANTONIO   I have.
DELIO
Make use then of this forced occasion.
Give out that Bosola hath poisoned her   170
With these apricots: that will give some colour
For her keeping close.
ANTONIO   Fie, fie, the physicians
Will then flock to her.
DELIO   For that you may pretend
She'll use some prepared antidote of her own,
Lest the physicians should re-poison her.   175

---

152 *farthingales* hooped petticoats
154 *apparently* clearly
155 *springal* stripling

ANTONIO

I am lost in amazement. I know not what to think on't.

Exeunt

[Act II,] Scene ii

[*Enter* BOSOLA]

BOSOLA

So, so: there's no question but her tetchiness, and most
vulturous eating of the apricots, are apparent signs of
breeding.

[*Enter* OLD LADY]

Now?

OLD LADY

I am in haste, sir.   5

BOSOLA

There was a young waiting-woman had a monstrous desire
to see the glass-house –

OLD LADY

Nay, pray let me go –

BOSOLA

And it was only to know what strange instrument it was
should swell up a glass to the fashion of a woman's belly.   10

OLD LADY

I will hear no more of the glass-house, you are still abusing
women.

BOSOLA

Who I? No, only by the way, now and then, mention your
frailties. The orange tree bears ripe and green fruit and
blossoms altogether, and some of you give entertainment   15
for pure love; but more, for more precious reward. The

---

   0 s.d. ed. (SCENA. II. / *Bosola, old Lady, Antonio, Rodorigo, Grisolan: seruants,
     Delio, Cariola.* Q1)
   5 The Old Lady is in haste to act as midwife to the Duchess: entering by one door,
     she is crossing the stage to exit at another when Bosola blocks her way.
   7 *glass-house* glass factory: Webster alludes to the Blackfriars glass factory in *The
     White Devil*, I.ii.132.
  14 *bears* ed. (beare Q1)
  15 *altogether* both together, simultanously
     entertainment sexual pleasure
  16 *precious reward* gold

lusty spring smells well, but drooping autumn tastes well. If
we have the same golden showers that rained in the time of
Jupiter the Thunderer, you have the same Danaes still, to
hold up their laps to receive them. Didst thou never study   20
the mathematics?

OLD LADY
What's that, sir?

BOSOLA
Why, to know the trick how to make a many lines meet in
one centre. Go, go; give your foster-daughters good council: tell them that the devil takes delight to hang at a   25
woman's girdle like a false rusty watch, that she cannot
discern how the time passes.

[*Exit* OLD LADY]

[*Enter* ANTONIO, DELIO, RODERIGO, GRISOLAN]

ANTONIO
Shut up the court gates.

RODERIGO   Why sir, what's the danger?

ANTONIO
Shut up the posterns presently, and call
All the officers o'th'court.

GRISOLAN   I shall, instantly.   [*Exit*]   30

ANTONIO
Who keeps the key o'th'park gate?

RODERIGO   Forobosco.

ANTONIO
Let him bring't presently.

[*Exeunt* ANTONIO *and* RODERIGO]

[*Enter* SERVANTS]

SERVANT
Oh gentlemen o'th'court, the foulest treason!

BOSOLA
If that these apricots should be poisoned, now, without my
knowledge!   35

---

19 *Danaes* ed. (*Danes* Q1)
     Receiving Jupiter in the form of a shower of gold, Danae became a synonym for
     a mercenary woman. See I.i.240–1.
23–4 *many ... centre* Proverbial; as in Montaigne, *Essayes*, III.v, p. 514: 'a Centre
     whereto all lines come'.
29 *presently* at once

SERVANT
  There was taken even now a Switzer in the Duchess'
  bedchamber.
2 SERVANT
  A Switzer?
SERVANT
  With a pistol in his great codpiece!
BOSOLA
  Ha, ha, ha.   40
SERVANT
  The codpiece was the case for't.
2 SERVANT
  There was a cunning traitor: who would have searched his
  codpiece?
SERVANT
  True, if he had kept out of the ladies' chambers; and all the
  moulds of his buttons were leaden bullets.   45
2 SERVANT
  Oh wicked cannibal: a fire-lock in's codpiece?
SERVANT
  'Twas a French plot, upon my life!
2 SERVANT
  To see what the devil can do!

            [*Enter* ANTONIO, RODERIGO, GRISOLAN]

ANTONIO
  All the officers here?
SERVANTS   We are.
ANTONIO   Gentlemen,
  We have lost much plate, you know; and but this evening   50
  Jewels to the value of four thousand ducats
  Are missing in the Duchess' cabinet.
  Are the gates shut?
SERVANT   Yes.

---

39 *pistol … codpiece* The Elizabethan pronunciation of *pistol* omitted the medial 't'
    – so Kökeritz, *Shakespeare's Pronunciation* (1953), p. 135, making the pun on
    pizzle = penis clearer. The *codpiece*, no longer fashionable by 1612, was some-
    times exaggerated in size and ornamentation – Rabelais has a memorable pass-
    age on Gargantua's opulent codpiece. Perhaps the joke involves not only the
    exaggerated size of the codpiece but also the unduly modest resources of the
    Switzer in this department.
47 *French* Presumably alluding to the 'French disease', syphilis.
49 *All* Q1 (Are all Q4); *officers* Q2 (offices Q1)
52 *cabinet* private chamber

ANTONIO   'Tis the Duchess' pleasure
  Each officer be locked into his chamber
  Till the sun-rising, and to send the keys   55
  Of all their chests, and of their outward doors,
  Into her bedchamber: she is very sick.
RODERIGO
  At her pleasure.
ANTONIO
  She entreats you take't not ill. The innocent
  Shall be the more approved by it.   60
BOSOLA
  Gentleman o'th'wood-yard, where's your Switzer now?
SERVANT
  By this hand, 'twas credibly reported by one o'th'Black-
  guard.

        [*Exeunt all but* DELIO *and* ANTONIO]

DELIO
  How fares it with the Duchess?
ANTONIO   She's exposed
  Unto the worst of torture, pain, and fear.   65
DELIO
  Speak to her all happy comfort.
ANTONIO
  How I do play the fool with mine own danger!
  You are this night, dear friend, to post to Rome,
  My life lies in your service.
DELIO   Do not doubt me.
ANTONIO
  Oh, 'tis far from me: and yet fear presents me   70
  Somewhat that looks like danger.
DELIO   Believe it,
  'Tis but the shadow of your fear, no more:
  How superstitiously we mind our ends:
  The throwing down salt, or crossing of a hare,
  Bleeding at nose, the stumbling of a horse   75
  Or singing of a cricket, are of power
  To daunt whole man in us. Sir, fare you well:
  I wish you all the joys of a blessed father

---

61 *Gentleman ... wood-yard* Bosola is clearly mocking the Servant's first words
    (line 33 and 36 above), so presumably the *wood-yard* has base and menial
    associations, like the next line's joke on *Black-guard* = scullions and greasy turn-
    spits.
71 *looks* Q2 (looke Q1)
77 *whole man* resolution

And, for my faith, lay this unto your breast:
Old friends, like old swords, still are trusted best.   [*Exit*]   80

[*Enter* CARIOLA]

CARIOLA
Sir, you are the happy father of a son.
Your wife commends him to you.
ANTONIO   Blessed comfort:
For heaven' sake tend her well. I'll presently
Go set a figure for's nativity.

Exeunt

[Act II,] Scene iii

[*Enter* BOSOLA *with a dark lantern*]

BOSOLA
Sure I did hear a woman shriek: list, ha?
And the sound came, if I received it right,
From the Duchess' lodgings. There's some stratagem
In the confining all our courtiers
To their several wards. I must have part of it,   5
My intelligence will freeze else. List again:
It may be 'twas the melancholy bird,
Best friend of silence, and of solitariness,
The owl, that screamed so –

[*Enter* ANTONIO, *with a horoscope*]

Ha? Antonio?

ANTONIO
I heard some noise: who's there? What art thou? Speak.   10

---

80 s.d. Q4 adds *with a Child*, but this is superfluous: Cariola's appearance is
    momentary and the dramatic function is not to display the child but to prompt
    Antonio to make the horoscope, since this is the focus of the next piece of plot.
84 *set ... nativity* cast his horoscope

 0 s.d. ed. (SCENA. III. / *Bosola, Antonio.* Q1; *Bosola, Antonio, with a dark
    lanthorn* Q4)
    dark lantern A lantern with an arrangement for concealing its light. On the
    Elizabethan stage the conventional signal that a scene takes place by night was
    for actors to carry a light. A lantern features again in V.iv.50ff., offering an
    ironic comment on Bosola's nocturnal and murky career in the play.
 9 s.d. ed. (Enter *Antonio,* with a Candle his sword drawn Q4)

BOSOLA
  Antonio? Put not your face nor body
  To such a forced expression of fear;
  I am Bosola, your friend.
ANTONIO   Bosola?
  [*Aside*] This mole does undermine me – heard you not
  A noise even now?
BOSOLA   From whence?
ANTONIO   From the Duchess' lodging.   15
BOSOLA
  Not I. Did you?
ANTONIO   I did, or else I dreamed.
BOSOLA
  Let's walk towards it.
ANTONIO   No. It may be 'twas
  But the rising of the wind.
BOSOLA   Very likely.
  Methinks 'tis very cold, and yet you sweat.
  You look wildly.
ANTONIO   I have been setting a figure   20
  For the Duchess' jewels.
BOSOLA   Ah: and how falls your question?
  Do you find it radical?
ANTONIO   What's that to you?
  'Tis rather to be questioned what design,
  When all men were commanded to their lodgings,
  Makes you a night-walker.
BOSOLA   In sooth I'll tell you: 25
  Now all the court's asleep, I thought the devil
  Had least to do here. I came to say my prayers,
  And if it do offend you I do so,
  You are a fine courtier.
ANTONIO [*Aside*]   This fellow will undo me. –
  You gave the Duchess apricots today,   30
  Pray heaven they were not poisoned.

20–1 *setting … jewels* Recourse to astrology supposedly enabled the discovery of lost
    goods. Antonio backs up this lie by referring to his earlier – false – claim (see
    II.ii.50ff.) that jewels had been stolen.
22 *radical* fit to be judged
25 *night-walker* nocturnal rogue or criminal
31–3 ed. (Pray … poysond? / Poysond? … figge / For … imputation. / Traitors …
    confident, / Till … Q1)

BOSOLA   Poisoned?
  A Spanish fig for the imputation.
ANTONIO
  Traitors are ever confident till they
  Are discovered. There were jewels stolen too.
  In my conceit none are to be suspected   35
  More than yourself.
BOSOLA   You are a false steward.
ANTONIO
  Saucy slave, I'll pull thee up by the roots!
BOSOLA
  May be the ruin will crush you to pieces.
ANTONIO
  You are an impudent snake indeed, sir!
  Are you scarce warm and do you show your sting?   40
[BOSOLA
  …]
ANTONIO
  You libel well, sir.
BOSOLA   No, sir. Copy it out
  And I will set my hand to't.
ANTONIO [*Aside*]   My nose bleeds.

        [*Takes out handkerchief and drops paper*]

  One that were superstitious would count
  This ominous, when it merely comes by chance: 45
  Two letters that are wrought here for my name
  Are drowned in blood:
  Mere accident. [*Aloud*] For you, sir, I'll take order:

---

32 *Spanish fig* An indecent gesture, thrusting the thumb between the first two fingers
    – and with a pun on the other meaning, poison (as in *The White Devil*, IV.ii.60).
41 s.p. *BOSOLA* ed. (not in Q1). In Q1 two consecutive speeches are given to
    Antonio, clearly an error: presumably the compositor or scribe accidentally
    omitted a speech by Bosola, one provoking Antonio's angry response in the next
    line.
42–3 *Copy … to't* If Antonio will write down the supposed libel Bosola will sign it.
42–4 ed. (You … (sir.) / No (sir,) / Copy … to't. / My … count Q1)
43 s.d. Developed from the implications in the text: the two letters are *wrought*
    (46), that is, embroidered, *here*, in the handkerchief with which Antonio
    stanches his nose bleed. Antonio drops *a paper* – identified by Bosola as the
    horoscope in line 57 – and it is simple and plausible that he does so when get-
    ting out his handkerchief (as was done in the Sadlers Wells production of 1850).
    Webster's use of the handkerchief is no doubt intended to recall *Othello* – both
    the likeness and difference are significant. See Introduction pp. xvi–vii.
47–8 ed. (one line Q1)

I'th'morn you shall be safe.[*Aside*] 'Tis that must colour
Her lying in: [*Aloud*] sir, this door you pass not.   50
I do not hold it fit that you come near
The Duchess' lodgings till you have quit yourself.
'The great are like the base, nay, they are the same,
When they seek shameful ways to avoid shame'.   *Exit*

BOSOLA

Antonio here about did drop a paper: 55
Some of your help, false friend:

          [*Searches with the lantern and finds paper*]

                    – oh, here it is.
What's here? A child's nativity calculated?
[*Reads*] *The Duchess was delivered of a son, 'tween the*
          hours twelve and one, in the night, Anno Dom: 1504,
          (that's this year) *decimo nono Decembris,* (that's this   60
          night) *taken according to the meridian of Malfi* (that's
          our Duchess: happy discovery). *The Lord of the first*
          house, being combust in the ascendant, signifies short
          life; and Mars being in a human sign, joined to the tail of
          the Dragon, in the eighth house, doth threaten a violent   65
          death. Caetera non scrutantur.
Why now 'tis most apparent. This precise fellow
Is the Duchess' bawd. I have it to my wish.
This is a parcel of intelligency
Our courtiers were cased up for. It needs must follow   70
That I must be committed on pretence

---

56 *false friend* The dark lantern.

58–66 As it turns out, this first-born child alone survives at the end of the play – but
          for how much longer? The prediction for a short life and a violent death remains;
          Caetera non scrutantur ('The rest is not examined') means only that the horo-
          scope has not been completed, not that its validity is uncertain. Webster's main
          interest is in what the astrological terminology can contribute to the general
          atmosphere of menace; the horoscope is implausible, astrologically speaking:
          NCW refer to J. C. Eade, *The Forgotten Sky* (1984), pp. 188–9.

62 *Lord ... house* See II.i.97n. This planet was supposed to be particularly influen-
          tial in the life of the child then born.

63 *combust* burnt up; this signifies a planet positioned within 8 degrees of the sun,
          whereby its influence is destroyed.

64 *human sign* Aquarius, Gemini, Virgo or Sagittarius

64–5 *tail ... Dragon* This lay where the moon traverses the ecliptic in its descent. It
          had a sinister influence.

65 *eighth* ed. (eight Q1); *eighth house* This regularly signified death.

67 *precise* strict, puritanical

70 *cased* ed. (caside Q1)

Of poisoning her, which I'll endure, and laugh at.
If one could find the father now: but that
Time will discover. Old Castruchio
I'th'morning posts to Rome; by him I'll send   75
A letter that shall make her brothers' galls
O'erflow their livers. This was a thrifty way.
'Though lust do masque in ne'er so strange disguise
She's oft found witty, but is never wise'.   [*Exit*]

[Act II,] Scene iv

[*Enter* CARDINAL *and* JULIA]

CARDINAL
Sit: thou art my best of wishes. Prithee tell me
What trick didst thou invent to come to Rome
Without thy husband.
JULIA   Why, my lord, I told him
I came to visit an old anchorite
Here, for devotion.
CARDINAL   Thou art a witty false one –   5
I mean, to him.
JULIA   You have prevailed with me
Beyond my strongest thoughts; I would not now
Find you inconstant.
CARDINAL   Do not put thyself
To such a voluntary torture, which proceeds
Out of your own guilt.
JULIA   How, my lord?   10
CARDINAL
You fear my constancy because you have approved
Those giddy and wild turnings in yourself.
JULIA
Did you e'er find them?

---

0 s.d. ed. (SCENA. IIII. / *Cardinall, and Iulia, Seruant, and Delio.* Q1)

1 *Sit* Orazio Busino (7 Feb 1618) reports seeing a performance where the Cardinal,
   presumably at this point, was shown 'with a harlot on his knee'. Recent productions have developed such possibilities further: in the Manchester Royal
   Exchange production 1980 the couple mimed sexual coition before speaking, in
   the RSC production of 1989/90 Julia advanced on the Cardinal, raising her skirts
   by degrees before sitting astride a chair to display her legs to him.

10 ed. (Out ... guilt. / How ... Lord? / Q1)

12 *turnings* ed. (turning Q1)

CARDINAL   Sooth, generally, for women,
  A man might strive to make glass malleable
  Ere he should make them fixed.
JULIA   So, my lord.   15
CARDINAL
  We had need go borrow that fantastic glass
  Invented by Galileo the Florentine
  To view another spacious world i'th'moon,
  And look to find a constant woman there.
JULIA
  This is very well, my lord.
CARDINAL   Why do you weep?   20
  Are tears your justification? The self-same tears
  Will fall into your husband's bosom, lady,
  With a loud protestation that you love him
  Above the world. Come, I'll love you wisely,
  That's jealously, since I am very certain   25
  You cannot me make cuckold.
JULIA   I'll go home
  To my husband.
CARDINAL   You may thank me, lady:
  I have taken you off your melancholy perch,
  Bore you upon my fist, and showed you game,
  And let you fly at it. I pray thee kiss me.   30
  When thou wast with thy husband thou wast watched
  Like a tame elephant – still you are to thank me –
  Thou hadst only kisses from him, and high feeding,
  But what delight was that? 'Twas just like one
  That hath a little fingering on the lute,   35
  Yet cannot tune it – still you are to thank me.
JULIA
  You told me of a piteous wound i'th'heart
  And a sick liver, when you wooed me first,
  And spake like one in physic.

                      [*Knocking*]

16 *fantastic glass* The telescope built by Galileo in 1609.

28–30 *perch ... it* As if she were a falcon.

30 *thee* ed. (the Q1)

31–2 *watched ... elephant* The comparison of Julia to an elephant is grotesque,
    with *tame* implying 'sexually frustrated'; *watched* could mean 'tamed by being
    kept awake' and also 'looked at' (like the real elephant put on public exhibition
    in London in 1594, which attracted great attention).

38 *liver* The seat of love and the passions.

CARDINAL   Who's that?
Rest firm: for my affection to thee,   40
Lightning moves slow to't.

[*Enter* SERVANT]

SERVANT   Madam, a gentleman
That's come post from Malfi, desires to see you.
CARDINAL
Let him enter, I'll withdraw.   *Exit*
SERVANT   He says
Your husband Old Castruchio is come to Rome,
Most pitifully tired with riding post.   [*Exit*]   45

[*Enter* DELIO]

JULIA
Signior Delio? [*Aside*] 'Tis one of my old suitors.
DELIO
I was bold to come and see you.
JULIA   Sir, you are welcome.
DELIO
Do you lie here?
JULIA   Sure, your own experience
Will satisfy you no, our Roman prelates
Do not keep lodging for ladies.
DELIO   Very well: 50
I have brought you no commendations from your husband,
For I know none by him.
JULIA   I hear he's come to Rome?
DELIO
I never knew man and beast, of a horse and a knight,
So weary of each other; if he had had a good back
He would have undertook to have borne his horse,   55
His breech was so pitifully sore.
JULIA   Your laughter
Is my pity.
DELIO   Lady, I know not whether
You want money, but I have brought you some.
JULIA
From my husband?
DELIO   No, from mine own allowance.
JULIA
I must hear the condition ere I be bound to take it.   60
DELIO
Look on't, 'tis gold, hath it not a fine colour?

47 *you* ed. (your Q1)

JULIA
  I have a bird more beautiful.
DELIO
  Try the sound on't.
JULIA   A lute-string far exceeds it,
  It hath no smell, like cassia or civet,
  Nor is it physical, though some fond doctors   65
  Persuade us seeth't in cullisses; I'll tell you,
  This is a creature bred by –

            [*Enter* SERVANT]

SERVANT   Your husband's come,
  Hath delivered a letter to the Duke of Calabria that,
  To my thinking, hath put him out of his wits.   [*Exit*]
JULIA
  Sir, you hear: 70
  Pray let me know your business, and your suit,
  As briefly as can be.
DELIO   With good speed. I would wish you,
  At such time as you are non-resident
  With your husband, my mistress.
JULIA
  Sir, I'll go ask my husband if I shall,   75
  And straight return your answer.   *Exit*
DELIO   Very fine.
  Is this her wit, or honesty, that speaks thus?
  I heard one say the Duke was highly moved
  With a letter sent from Malfi. I do fear
  Antonio is betrayed. How fearfully   80
  Shows his ambition now: unfortunate Fortune!
  'They pass through whirlpools, and deep woes do shun,
  Who the event weigh, ere the action's done'.   *Exit*

---

65 *physical* used as medicine
66 *seeth't* ed. (seeth's Q1)
   cullisses broths
77–80 This soliloquy seems to suggest that Delio is on a mission of espionage, and
    possibly plans to manipulate Julia (indeed in V.ii Bosola succeeds in doing this);
    but no more emerges of the present intrigue. This may be deliberate on Webster's
    part, and designed to create an atmosphere of secret plotting.
82 *pass through* successfully cross

[Act II,] Scene v

[*Enter*] CARDINAL, *and* FERDINAND *with a letter*

FERDINAND
　I have this night digged up a mandrake.
CARDINAL   Say you?
FERDINAND
　And I am grown mad with't.
CARDINAL   What's the prodigy?
FERDINAND
　Read there: a sister damned, she's loose i'th'hilts,
　Grown a notorious strumpet!
CARDINAL   Speak lower.
FERDINAND   Lower?
　Rogues do not whisper't now, but seek to publish't,   5
　As servants do the bounty of their lords,
　Aloud; and with a covetous searching eye
　To mark who note them. Oh confusion seize her!
　She hath had most cunning bawds to serve her turn,
　And more secure conveyances for lust   10
　Than towns of garrison, for service.
CARDINAL   Is't possible?
　Can this be certain?
FERDINAND   Rhubarb, oh, for rhubarb
　To purge this choler! Here's the cursèd day
　To prompt my memory, and here it shall stick
　Till of her bleeding heart I make a sponge   15
　To wipe it out.
CARDINAL   Why do you make yourself
　So wild a tempest?
FERDINAND   Would I could be one,
　That I might toss her palace 'bout her ears,
　Root up her goodly forests, blast her meads,

0 s.d. ed. (SCENA V. / *Cardinall, and Ferdinand, with a letter.* Q1)
1 *digged* Q1b (dig Q1a)
　mandrake The forked root of the plant mandragora, supposedly resembling a
　man, gave rise to the superstition that when dug up it emitted a shriek which
　induced madness.
2 *prodigy* ed. (progedy Q1)
3 *loose i'th'hilts* unchaste
11 *service* supplies (including sexual services)
12 *rhubarb* A recognised antidote to choler.

And lay her general territory as waste   20
As she hath done her honours.
CARDINAL   Shall our blood,
  The royal blood of Aragon and Castile,
  Be thus attainted?
FERDINAND   Apply desperate physic!
  We must not now use balsamum, but fire,
  The smarting cupping glass, for that's the mean   25
  To purge infected blood, such blood as hers.
  There is a kind of pity in mine eye,
  I'll give it to my handkercher –
        [*He wipes away the tears with a handkerchief*]
                        and now 'tis here,
  I'll bequeath this to her bastard.
CARDINAL   What to do?
FERDINAND
  Why, to make soft lint for his mother's wounds,   30
  When I have hewed her to pieces.
CARDINAL   Cursed creature!
  Unequal nature, to place women's hearts
  So far upon the left side.
FERDINAND   Foolish men,
  That e'er will trust their honour in a bark
  Made of so slight weak bullrush as is woman,   35
  Apt every minute to sink it!
CARDINAL   Thus
  Ignorance, when it hath purchased honour,
  It cannot wield it.
FERDINAND   Methinks I see her laughing –
  Excellent hyena! Talk to me somewhat quickly,
  Or my imagination will carry me   40
  To see her in the shameful act of sin.
CARDINAL   With whom?
FERDINAND
  Happily with some strong-thighed bargeman;

23 *attainted* The Cardinal intends the legal term referring to lineage stained or cor-
    rupted; Ferdinand takes it literally, referring to blood infected with disease (with
    the added sense of *blood* = passion).
28 s.d. Webster stresses the action in lines 27–8, ironically recalling Antonio's fatal
    use of his handkerchief for the nosebleed in II.iii.
30 *mother's* ed. (mother Q1)
33 *left* Probably to be understood figuratively, as sinister, not right (see III.i.28–9).
36–7 ed. (Thus / Ignorance … honour Q1)

Or one o'th'woodyard that can quoit the sledge
Or toss the bar; or else some lovely squire
That carries coals up to her privy lodgings.   45
CARDINAL
  You fly beyond your reason.
FERDINAND   Go to, mistress,
  'Tis not your whore's milk that shall quench my wild-fire,
  But your whore's blood!
CARDINAL
  How idly shows this rage, which carries you
  As men conveyed by witches through the air   50
  On violent whirlwinds! This intemperate noise
  Fitly resembles deaf men's shrill discourse,
  Who talk aloud, thinking all other men
  To have their imperfection.
FERDINAND   Have not you
  My palsy?
CARDINAL   Yes. I can be angry   55
  Without this rupture; there is not in nature
  A thing that makes man so deformed, so beastly,
  As doth intemperate anger. Chide yourself.
  You have diverse men who never yet expressed
  Their strong desire of rest, but by unrest –   60
  By vexing of themselves. Come, put yourself
  In tune.
FERDINAND So, I will only study to seem
  The thing I am not. I could kill her now
  In you, or in myself, for I do think
  It is some sin in us heaven doth revenge   65
  By her.
CARDINAL   Are you stark mad?
FERDINAND   I would have their bodies
  Burnt in a coal pit with the ventage stopped,
  That their cursed smoke might not ascend to heaven;
  Or dip the sheets they lie in, in pitch or sulphur,
  Wrap them in't and then light them like a match;   70
  Or else to boil their bastard to a cullis

---

43 *o'th'* ed. (th' Q1)
     quoit the sledge throw the hammer
45 *carries coals* With a subsidiary (proverbial) sense 'do any dirty or menial work'.
     privy lodgings private apartment (with puns on *privy* parts = genitals, and
     lodgings = sexual penetrations)
49–50 ed. (How ... rage / Which ... ayre Q1)
55 *palsy* the shaking palsy, involuntary tremors (*OED* sb 1a)
56 *rupture* Q1 (rapture conj. Dyce)

And give't his lecherous father to renew
The sin of his back.
CARDINAL   I'll leave you.
FERDINAND   Nay, I have done.
I am confident, had I been damned in hell
And should have heard of this, it would have put me   75
Into a cold sweat. In, in, I'll go sleep.
Till I know who leaps my sister, I'll not stir:
That known, I'll find scorpions to string my whips,
And fix her in a general eclipse.

                                                    Exeunt

Act III, Scene i

[*Enter* ANTONIO *and* DELIO]

ANTONIO
Our noble friend, my most beloved Delio,
Oh you have been a stranger long at court;
Came you along with the Lord Ferdinand?
DELIO
I did sir; and how fares your noble Duchess?
ANTONIO
Right fortunately well. She's an excellent   5
Feeder of pedigrees: since you last saw her,
She hath had two children more, a son, and daughter.
DELIO
Methinks 'twas yesterday – let me but wink
And not behold your face, which to mine eye
Is somewhat leaner, verily I should dream   10
It were within this half hour.
ANTONIO
You have not been in law, friend Delio,
Nor in prison, nor a suitor at the court,
Nor begged the reversion of some great man's place,
Nor troubled with an old wife, which doth make   15
Your time so insensibly hasten.

---

0 s.d. ed. (ACTVS III. SCENA I. / *Antonio, and Delio, Duchesse, Ferdinand,
    Bosola.* Q1)

2 Delio has been away in Rome since the end of II.ii.

10–11 A self-conscious allusion by Webster to the conventions of theatrical illusion,
    in which some two years must be imagined to have passed since II.ii – in per-
    formance time, certainly less than half an hour since.

DELIO   Pray sir tell me,
  Hath not this news arrived yet to the ear
  Of the Lord Cardinal?
ANTONIO   I fear it hath.
  The Lord Ferdinand that's newly come to court
  Doth bear himself right dangerously.
DELIO   Pray why?   20
ANTONIO
  He is so quiet that he seems to sleep
  The tempest out as dormice do in winter.
  Those houses that are haunted are most still
  Till the devil be up.
DELIO   What say the common people?
ANTONIO
  The common rabble do directly say   25
  She is a strumpet.
DELIO   And your graver heads,
  Which would be politic, what censure they?
ANTONIO
  They do observe I grow to infinite purchase
  The left-hand way, and all suppose the Duchess
  Would amend it if she could. For, say they,   30
  Great princes, though they grudge their officers
  Should have such large and unconfinèd means
  To get wealth under them, will not complain
  Lest thereby they should make them odious
  Unto the people; for other obligation –   35
  Of love, or marriage, between her and me –
  They never dream of.

      [*Enter* DUCHESS, FERDINAND *and* BOSOLA]

DELIO   The Lord Ferdinand
  Is going to bed.
FERDINAND   I'll instantly to bed,
  For I am weary. I am to bespeak
  A husband for you.

19ff. This discussion is clearly parallel to that between Delio and Antonio about
    good government in Act I, but here Antonio seems to be admitting that keeping
    the marriage secret has seriously weakened the Duchess as ruler, even without
    the new danger of Ferdinand's presence.

27 *be* ed. (he Q1)

28 *purchase* wealth

29 *left-hand* corrupt

37 *of* ed. (off Q1)

39 *bespeak* ed. (be be-speake Q1)

DUCHESS   For me, sir? Pray who is't?   40
FERDINAND
  The great Count Malateste.
DUCHESS   Fie upon him!
  A Count? He's a mere stick of sugar candy,
  You may look quite thorough him. When I choose
  A husband, I will marry for your honour.
FERDINAND
  You shall do well in't. – How is't, worthy Antonio?   45
DUCHESS
  But, sir, I am to have private conference with you
  About a scandalous report is spread
  Touching mine honour.
FERDINAND   Let me be ever deaf to't:
  One of Pasquil's paper bullets, court calumny,
  A pestilent air which princes' palaces   50
  Are seldom purged of. Yet, say that it were true:
  I pour it in your bosom, my fixed love
  Would strongly excuse, extenuate, nay deny
  Faults, were they apparent in you. Go be safe
  In your own innocency.
DUCHESS   Oh bless'd comfort,   55
  This deadly air is purged.

          Exeunt [all but FERDINAND *and* BOSOLA]

FERDINAND   Her guilt treads on
  Hot burning coulters. Now Bosola,
  How thrives our intelligence?
BOSOLA   Sir, uncertainly:
  'Tis rumoured she hath had three bastards, but
  By whom, we may go read i'th'stars.
FERDINAND   Why some   60
  Hold opinion all things are written there.
BOSOLA
  Yes, if we could find spectacles to read them.

---

49 *Pasquil's paper bullets* satires or lampoons (*Pasquin* or *Pasquil* became a popu-
    lar name for a satirist, following the custom in 16th century Rome of attaching
    lampoons to a statue named after one Pasquino or Pasquillo, a sharp-tongued
    schoolmaster or cobbler).

54 *were* ed. (where Q1)

56–7 *treads ... coulters* An ordeal decreed as a trial of chastity in Old English law;
    the mother of Edward the Confessor is reputed to have walked barefoot upon
    'nine coulters red hot'. The coulter is the cutting blade in front of a ploughshare.
    coulters ed. (cultures Q1)

I do suspect there hath been some sorcery
Used on the Duchess.
FERDINAND   Sorcery? To what purpose?
BOSOLA
To make her dote on some desertless fellow   65
She shames to acknowledge.
FERDINAND   Can your faith give way
To think there's power in potions or in charms
To make us love, whether we will or no?
BOSOLA
Most certainly.
FERDINAND
Away! These are mere gulleries, horrid things   70
Invented by some cheating mountebanks
To abuse us. Do you think that herbs or charms
Can force the will? Some trials have been made
In this foolish practice, but the ingredients
Were lenitive poisons, such as are of force   75
To make the patient mad; and straight the witch
Swears, by equivocation, they are in love.
The witchcraft lies in her rank blood. This night
I will force confession from her. You told me
You had got, within these two days, a false key   80
Into her bedchamber?
BOSOLA   I have.
FERDINAND   As I would wish.
BOSOLA
What do you intend to do?
FERDINAND   Can you guess?
BOSOLA   No.
FERDINAND
Do not ask then.
He that can compass me, and know my drifts,
May say he hath put a girdle 'bout the world   85
And sounded all her quicksands.
BOSOLA   I do not
Think so.

---

75 *lenitive poisons* drugs seemingly aphrodisiac but inducing madness. N. W.
Bawcutt in *MLR* 66, pp. 488–91, claims that Webster is recalling Shelton's
translation of *Don Quixote*, I.iii.8: 'poysons ... cause men runne mad, and in
the meane while perswade us they have force to make one love well'. Lucas notes
Webster in *Anything for a Quiet Life*, I.i.91, using *lenitive* to mean 'soothing',
but finds this goes oddly with *poisons*: is Webster guilty of false etymology, via
Latin *lenare* = to prostitute? The phrase could then mean 'violent aphrodisiac'.
87 ed. (Thinke so. / What ... pray? / That ... are / Q1)

FERDINAND   What do you think then, pray?
BOSOLA   That you are
  Your own chronicle too much, and grossly
  Flatter yourself.
FERDINAND   Give me thy hand, I thank thee.
  I never gave pension but to flatterers   90
  Till I entertained thee: farewell.
  'That friend a great man's ruin strongly checks,
  Who rails into his belief, all his defects'.

                                              Exeunt

[Act III,] Scene ii

[*Enter* DUCHESS, ANTONIO *and* CARIOLA]

DUCHESS
  Bring me the casket hither, and the glass.
  You get no lodging here tonight my lord.
ANTONIO
  Indeed I must persuade one.
DUCHESS   Very good.
  I hope in time 'twill grow into a custom
  That noblemen shall come with cap and knee   5
  To purchase a night's lodging of their wives.
ANTONIO
  I must lie here.
DUCHESS   Must? You are a Lord of Misrule.
ANTONIO
  Indeed, my rule is only in the night.
DUCHESS
  To what use will you put me?
ANTONIO   We'll sleep together.
DUCHESS
  Alas, what pleasure can two lovers find in sleep?   10
CARIOLA
  My lord, I lie with her often and I know
  She'll much disquiet you –

---

  0 s.d. ed. (SCENA. II. / *Dutchesse, Antonio, Cariola, Ferdinand, Bosola, Officers.* Q1)
     The Duchess will remove her jewellery and brush her hair in preparation for bed;
     candles or torches would indicate that it is night.
  7 *Misrule* ed. (Misse-rule Q); *Lord of Misrule* (1) Someone very young or of low
     degree, traditionally chosen to preside over feasts and revels at court, reversing
     the usual hierarchies (2) Punning on *Mis* / *Misse* = kept mistress.

ANTONIO   See, you are complained of –
CARIOLA
  For she's the sprawling'st bedfellow.
ANTONIO
  I shall like her the better for that.
CARIOLA
  Sir, shall I ask you a question?
ANTONIO   I pray thee Cariola.   15
CARIOLA
  Wherefore still when you lie with my lady
  Do you rise so early?
ANTONIO   Labouring men
  Count the clock oft'nest, Cariola,
  Are glad when their task's ended.
DUCHESS   I'll stop your mouth.
                    [*Kisses him*]
ANTONIO
  Nay, that's but one, Venus had two soft doves   20
  To draw her chariot: I must have another.
                    [*She kisses him*]
  When wilt thou marry, Cariola?
CARIOLA   Never, my lord.
ANTONIO
  Oh fie upon this single life! Forgo it:
  We read how Daphne, for her peevish flight,
  Became a fruitless bay-tree, Syrinx turn'd   25
  To the pale empty reed, Anaxarete
  Was frozen into marble, whereas those
  Which married, or proved kind unto their friends,
  Were by a gracious influence transshaped
  Into the olive, pomegranate, mulberry,   30
  Became flowers, precious stones or eminent stars.
CARIOLA
  This is a vain poetry; but I pray you tell me,
  If there were proposed me wisdom, riches, and beauty,
  In three several young men, which should I choose?
ANTONIO
  'Tis a hard question. This was Paris' case   35
  And he was blind in't, and there was great cause:
  For how was't possible he could judge right,

---

22 *Never* An ironically prophetic answer: this dialogue recalls *Antony and Cleopatra*, I.ii, where the Soothsayer converses with Charmian, Iras and Alexas.
24 *flight* ed. (slight Q1)
25 *Syrinx* ed. (*Siriux* Q1b, *Sirina* Q1a)
28 *friends* lovers

Having three amorous goddesses in view,
And they stark naked? 'Twas a motion
Were able to be-night the apprehension   40
Of the severest counsellor of Europe.
Now I look on both your faces so well formed
It puts me in mind of a question I would ask.

CARIOLA
What is't?

ANTONIO   I do wonder why hard-favoured ladies
For the most part keep worse-favoured waiting-women   45
To attend them, and cannot endure fair ones.

DUCHESS
Oh, that's soon answered.
Did you ever in your life know an ill painter
Desire to have his dwelling next door to the shop
Of an excellent picture-maker? 'Twould disgrace   50
His face-making, and undo him. – I prithee
When were we so merry? My hair tangles.

ANTONIO
[*Aside to* CARIOLA] Pray thee, Cariola, let's steal forth the room
And let her talk to herself. I have divers times
Served her the like, when she hath chafed extremely.   55
I love to see her angry. Softly Cariola.

Exeunt [ANTONIO *and* CARIOLA]

DUCHESS
Doth not the colour of my hair 'gin to change?
When I wax grey I shall have all the court
Powder their hair with arras, to be like me:

[*Enter* FERDINAND, *behind*]

You have cause to love me, I enter'd you into my heart   60
Before you would vouchsafe to call for the keys.
We shall one day have my brothers take you napping:
Methinks his presence, being now in court,

---

39 *motion* show

40 *apprehension* Q1b (approbation Q1a)

49 *his* Q1b (the Q1a)

56 s.d., 59 s.d. An ironic parallel with I.i.353–466 where, after hiding behind the arras, Cariola appears, surprising Antonio. Lucas unpersuasively suggests (in view of line 145 below) that here Webster intends Ferdinand to be seen 'above', crossing the upper stage before descending out of sight and then making this entrance on the main stage.

59 *arras* powdered orris-root, white and smelling of violets, used on the hair

Should make you keep your own bed; but you'll say
Love mixed with fear is sweetest. I'll assure you   65
You shall get no more children till my brothers
Consent to be your gossips. – Have you lost your tongue?

        [She sees FERDINAND]

'Tis welcome:
For know, whether I am doomed to live, or die,
I can do both like a prince.

       FERDINAND *gives her a poniard*

FERDINAND   Die then, quickly!   70
  Virtue, where art thou hid? What hideous thing
  Is it that doth eclipse thee?
DUCHESS   Pray sir hear me.
FERDINAND
  Or is it true thou art but a bare name,
  And no essential thing?
DUCHESS   Sir –
FERDINAND   Do not speak.
DUCHESS
  No sir: 75
  I will plant my soul in mine ears to hear you.
FERDINAND
  Oh most imperfect light of human reason,
  That mak'st so unhappy to foresee
  What we can least prevent, pursue thy wishes
  And glory in them: there's in shame no comfort   80
  But to be past all bounds and sense of shame.
DUCHESS
  I pray sir, hear me: I am married.
FERDINAND   So.
DUCHESS
  Happily, not to your liking; but for that,

---

67 *gossips* godparents for the children
67 s.d. The staging is especially powerful if the Duchess catches sight of Ferdinand
    in the mirror. There is a visual allusion to the Dance of Death, where the figure
    of Death arrests men and women of various ages and ranks, including youth-
    ful queens and duchesses. The mirror in such cases is an emblem of female
    vanity.
67–8 ed. (Consent … welcome / Q1)
69 s.d. Q1b (not in Q1a); *poniard* Presumably the dagger is his father's, the one
    with which he threatened the Duchess in I.i.323.
83 *Happily* Perhaps

Alas, your shears do come untimely now
To clip the bird's wings that's already flown.   85
Will you see my husband?
FERDINAND   Yes, if I could change
Eyes with a basilisk.
DUCHESS   Sure, you came hither
By his confederacy.
FERDINAND   The howling of a wolf
Is music to thee, screech owl, prithee peace.
What e'er thou art that hast enjoyed my sister –   90
For I am sure thou hear'st me – for thine own sake
Let me not know thee. I came hither prepared
To work thy discovery, yet am now persuaded
It would beget such violent effects
As would damn us both. I would not for ten millions   95
I had beheld thee, therefore use all means
I never may have knowledge of thy name.
Enjoy thy lust still, and a wretched life,
On that condition; and for thee, vile woman,
If thou do wish thy lecher may grow old   100
In thy embracements, I would have thee build
Such a room for him as our anchorites
To holier use inhabit. Let not the sun
Shine on him till he's dead, let dogs and monkeys
Only converse with him, and such dumb things   105
To whom nature denies use to sound his name.
Do not keep a paraquito lest she learn it.
If thou do love him cut out thine own tongue
Lest it bewray him.
DUCHESS   Why might not I marry?
I have not gone about in this to create   110
Any new world or custom.
FERDINAND   Thou art undone;
And thou hast ta'en that massy sheet of lead
That hid thy husband's bones, and folded it
About my heart.
DUCHESS   Mine bleeds for't.
FERDINAND   Thine? Thy heart?

86–7 ed. (Will ... husband? / Yes, if I / Could ... Basilisque: / Sure ... hither / Q1)
87 *basilisk* a mythical kind of serpent: its breath, or the sight of it, was supposedly
     fatal.
88 *confederacy* ed. (consideracy Q1)
89 *to thee* compared to thee

What should I name't, unless a hollow bullet   115
Filled with unquenchable wild-fire?
DUCHESS   You are in this
  Too strict, and were you not my princely brother
  I would say too wilful. My reputation
  Is safe.
FERDINAND   Dost thou know what reputation is?
  I'll tell thee – to small purpose, since th'instruction   120
  Comes now too late.
  Upon a time Reputation, Love, and Death
  Would travel o'er the world; and it was concluded
  That they should part, and take three several ways:
  Death told them they should find him in great battles   125
  Or cities plagued with plagues; Love gives them counsel
  To enquire for him 'mongst unambitious shepherds,
  Where dowries were not talked of, and sometimes
  'Mongst quiet kindred that had nothing left
  By their dead parents. 'Stay', quoth Reputation,   130
  'Do not forsake me: for it is my nature
  If once I part from any man I meet
  I am never found again'; and so for you:
  You have shook hands with Reputation
  And made him invisible. So fare you well.   135
  I will never see you more.
DUCHESS   Why should only I
  Of all the other princes of the world
  Be cased up like a holy relic? I have youth,
  And a little beauty.
FERDINAND   So you have some virgins
  That are witches. I will never see thee more.   *Exit*   140

         Enter ANTONIO *with a pistol* [*and* CARIOLA]

DUCHESS
  You saw this apparition?
ANTONIO   Yes, we are
  Betrayed. How came he hither? I should turn
  This to thee, for that.
            [*Points the pistol at* CARIOLA]
CARIOLA   Pray sir do: and when
  That you have cleft my heart you shall read there
  Mine innocence.

---

115   *What ... unless* What else should I call it but
115   *hollow bullet* cannon-ball filled with explosive, not the older type which was a
     solid iron ball
118   *too* ed. (to Q1)
134   *shook* Q1c (shooked Q1a, Q1b)

DUCHESS   That gallery gave him entrance.   145
ANTONIO
  I would this terrible thing would come again
  That, standing on my guard, I might relate
  My warrantable love. Ha, what means this?
DUCHESS
  He left this with me –
          She shows the poniard
ANTONIO   And it seems did wish
  You would use it on yourself?
DUCHESS   His action   150
  Seemed to intend so much.
ANTONIO   This hath a handle to't
  As well as a point, turn it towards him
  And so fasten the keen edge in his rank gall.

              [*Knocking*]

  How now? Who knocks? More earthquakes?
DUCHESS   I stand
  As if a mine beneath my feet were ready   155
  To be blown up.
CARIOLA   'Tis Bosola.
DUCHESS   Away!
  Oh misery, methinks unjust actions
  Should wear these masks and curtains, and not we:
  You must instantly part hence: I have fashioned it already.

              Exit ANTONIO

          [*Enter* BOSOLA]

BOSOLA
  The Duke your brother is ta'en up in a whirlwind: 160
  Hath took horse and's rid post to Rome.
DUCHESS   So late?
BOSOLA
  He told me as he mounted into th'saddle
  You were undone.
DUCHESS   Indeed I am very near it.

---

145 *gallery* It is not likely that Webster intends the audience to visualise the *gallery*
    as the stage's upper playing space. The play makes numerous references to
    specific rooms and parts of palaces and houses in the named cities – Malfi, Rome,
    Loretto, Ancona, Milan. As with IV.ii.31 where the Duchess' portrait is said to
    hang in the gallery, the effect here is impressionistic rather than exactly realistic
    in the nineteenth-century manner of Ibsen.

BOSOLA
  What's the matter?
DUCHESS   Antonio, the master of our household
  Hath dealt so falsely with me in's accounts.   165
  My brother stood engaged with me for money
  Ta'en up of certain Neapolitan Jews,
  And Antonio lets the bonds be forfeit.
BOSOLA
  Strange! [*Aside*] This is cunning.
DUCHESS   And hereupon
  My brother's bills at Naples are protested   170
  Against. Call up our officers.
BOSOLA   I shall.   *Exit*

                [*Enter* ANTONIO]

DUCHESS
  The place that you must fly to is Ancona:
  Hire a house there. I'll send after you
  My treasure and my jewels. Our weak safety
  Runs upon enginous wheels, short syllables   175
  Must stand for periods. I must now accuse you
  Of such a feigned crime as Tasso calls
  Magnanima mensogna, a noble lie,
  'Cause it must shield our honours. Hark, they are coming!

          [*Enter* BOSOLA *and* OFFICERS]

ANTONIO
  Will your grace hear me?   180

164–71 A similar feeble excuse, of theft, to that in II.ii.50ff., where Bosola was also
    present.
166–7 *stood ... up* was security for money I borrowed
168 *lets ... forfeit* Presumably by failing to make the payments.
170–1 *bills ... Against* promissory notes are not accepted
172 But see below 299–305 and n.
175 *enginous* ed. (engenous Q1)
    enginous wheels Like those of a clock where a small, almost imperceptible move-
    ment produces obvious motion in the hands (Brennan).
177 *Tasso* Alluding to *Gerusalemme Liberata*, 2.22, where Soprina falsely confesses
    taking a statue of the Virgin Mary from a mosque, in order to prevent wholesale
    persecution of her fellow Christians.

DUCHESS

   I have got well by you: you have yielded me
   A million of loss; I am like to inherit
   The people's curses for your stewardship.
   You had the trick in audit time to be sick
   Till I had signed your *Quietus*; and that cured you   185
   Without help of a doctor. Gentlemen,
   I would have this man be an example to you all,
   So shall you hold my favour. I pray let him,
   For h'as done that, alas, you would not think of,
   And, because I intend to be rid of him,   190
   I mean not to publish. – Use your fortune elsewhere.

ANTONIO

   I am strongly armed to brook my overthrow,
   As commonly men bear with a hard year.
   I will not blame the cause on't but do think
   The necessity of my malevolent star   195
   Procures this, not her humour. Oh the inconstant
   And rotten ground of service you may see:
   'Tis ev'n like him that in a winter night
   Takes a long slumber o'er a dying fire
   As loth to part from't, yet parts thence as cold   200
   As when he first sat down.

DUCHESS   We do confiscate,
   Towards the satisfying of your accounts,
   All that you have.

ANTONIO   I am all yours: and 'tis very fit
   All mine should be so.

DUCHESS   So, sir; you have your pass.

ANTONIO

   You may see, gentlemen, what 'tis to serve   205
   A prince with body and soul.   *Exit*

BOSOLA

   Here's an example for extortion! What moisture is drawn
   out of the sea, when foul weather comes, pours down and
   runs into the sea again.

DUCHESS

   I would know what are your opinions of this Antonio.   210

181 *got well* This double entendre is the first of a series down to 206 in which the
    Duchess and Antonio covertly affirm their love. For a memorable instance in
    Shakespeare see *Romeo and Juliet*, III.v.68-102.
188 *let him* let him go free (but *let* could also mean 'stop')
200 *As loth* Q1c (A-loth Q1a, Q1b)
210 ed. (as verse Q1)

2 OFFICER

He could not abide to see a pig's head gaping; I thought
your grace would find him a Jew.

3 OFFICER

I would you had been his officer, for your own sake.

4 OFFICER

You would have had more money.

1 OFFICER

He stopped his ears with black wool, and to those came to   215
him for money, said he was thick of hearing.

2 OFFICER

Some said he was an hermaphrodite, for he could not abide
a woman.

4 OFFICER

How scurvy proud he would look when the treasury was
full! Well, let him go.   220

1 OFFICER

Yes, and the chippings of the butt'ry fly after him, to scour
his gold chain!

DUCHESS

Leave us.

Exeunt [OFFICERS]

[*To* BOSOLA] What do you think of these?

BOSOLA

That these are rogues that, in's prosperity,
But to have waited on his fortune, could have wished   225
His dirty stirrup riveted through their noses
And followed after's mule like a bear in a ring;
Would have prostituted their daughters to his lust,
Made their first born intelligencers, thought none happy

211–12 *pig's head ... Jew* A crudely racist way of saying Antonio is financially
    untrustworthy – the sycophantic Officer takes the hint of line 167's reference to
    Neapolitan Jews. Webster is again drawing on *Merchant of Venice*: in IV.i
    Shylock refers twice to one who 'cannot abide a gaping pig'. A Christian proverb
    is 'Invite not a Jew either to pig or pork' (Tilley P310).
221 *chipping*s parings of the crust of a loaf
222 *gold chain* The steward's official chain of office. In *Twelfth Night*, II.iii.119-20,
    Malvolio is mockingly told to rub his chain 'with crumbs'.
224ff. Bosola's praise of Antonio is an elaborate and over-extended ploy, yet it per-
    suades the Duchess to confide in him. Perhaps she is so surprised to hear praise
    from this wonted malcontent that she is disarmed; but even if Bosola's estima-
    tion of Antonio is sincere, he continues to serve Ferdinand.
229 *intelligencers* Q1c (and Intelligencers Q1a, Q1b)

But such as were born under his blessed planet   230
And wore his livery; and do these lice drop off now?
Well, never look to have the like again.
He hath left a sort of flatt'ring rogues behind him:
Their doom must follow. Princes pay flatterers
In their own money: flatterers dissemble their vices,   235
And they dissemble their lies: that's justice.
Alas, poor gentleman.
DUCHESS
Poor? He hath amply filled his coffers.
BOSOLA
Sure he was too honest. Pluto the god of riches,
When he's sent by Jupiter to any man,   240
He goes limping, to signify that wealth
That comes on god's name, comes slowly; but when he's
    sent
On the devil's errand he rides post and comes in by scuttles.
Let me show you what a most unvalued jewel
You have in a wanton humour thrown away   245
To bless the man shall find him. He was an excellent
Courtier, and most faithful, a soldier that thought it
As beastly to know his own value too little
As devilish to acknowledge it too much;
Both his virtue and form deserved a far better fortune;   250
His discourse rather delighted to judge itself than show
    itself,
His breast was filled with all perfection
And yet it seemed a private whisp'ring room,
It made so little noise of't.
DUCHESS   But he was basely descended.
BOSOLA
Will you make yourself a mercenary herald,   255
Rather to examine men's pedigrees than virtues?
You shall want him,
For know: an honest statesman to a prince
Is like a cedar planted by a spring;
The spring bathes the tree's root, the grateful tree   260
Rewards it with his shadow. You have not done so:

---

239 *Pluto* The god of riches was Plutus, whereas Pluto was god of the underworld.
    Lucas suggests that the link of association was that wealth came from under-
    ground.
243 *On* ed. (One Q1)
    scuttles The meaning is uncertain: 'short hurried runs' (*OED*) or 'large baskets'
    (Brown).
244 *unvalued* priceless, very valuable

I would sooner swim to the Bermoothes on
Two politicians' rotten bladders, tied
Together with an intelligencer's heart-string,
Than depend on so changeable a prince's favour!   265
Fare thee well, Antonio: since the malice of the world
Would needs down with thee, it cannot be said yet
That any ill happened unto thee,
Considering thy fall was accompanied with virtue.

DUCHESS
Oh, you render me excellent music.

BOSOLA   Say you?   270

DUCHESS
This good one that you speak of is my husband.

BOSOLA
Do I not dream? Can this ambitious age
Have so much goodness in't as to prefer
A man merely for worth, without these shadows
Of wealth and painted honours? Possible?   275

DUCHESS
I have had three children by him.

BOSOLA   Fortunate lady,
For you have made your private nuptial bed
The humble and fair seminary of peace,
No question but many an unbeneficed scholar
Shall pray for you, for this deed, and rejoice   280
That some preferment in the world can yet
Arise from merit. The virgins of your land
That have no dowries, shall hope your example
Will raise them to rich husbands; should you want
Soldiers 'twould make the very Turks and Moors   285
Turn Christians and serve you, for this act;
Last, the neglected poets of your time,
In honour of this trophy of a man
Raised by that curious engine, your white hand,
Shall thank you, in your grave, for't, and make that   290
More reverend than all the cabinets
Of living princes. For Antonio,
His fame shall likewise flow from many a pen
When heralds shall want coats to sell to men.

262–4 ed. (I ... Politisians / Rotten ... hart-string / Q1)

262 *Bermoothes* The reports of the wreck of Sir George Somers on the Bermudas in 1609
     were topical and famous, and were used by Shakespeare in writing *The Tempest*.

289 *curious* delicate, dainty

294 The sale of honours (involving the devising of coats of arms) was a subject of
     much attack by satirists in the early Jacobean age.

DUCHESS
As I taste comfort in this friendly speech,   295
So would I find concealment.
BOSOLA
Oh the secret of my prince,
Which I will wear on th'inside of my heart!
DUCHESS
You shall take charge of all my coin, and jewels,
And follow him, for he retires himself   300
To Ancona.
BOSOLA   So.
DUCHESS   Whither, within few days,
I mean to follow thee.
BOSOLA   Let me think:
I would wish your grace to feign a pilgrimage
To Our Lady of Loretto, scarce seven leagues
From fair Ancona: so may you depart   305
Your country with more honour, and your flight
Will seem a princely progress, retaining
Your usual train about you.
DUCHESS   Sir, your direction
Shall lead me by the hand.
CARIOLA   In my opinion
She were better progress to the baths   310
At Lucca, or go visit the Spa
In Germany, for, if you will believe me,
I do not like this jesting with religion,
This feigned pilgrimage.
DUCHESS   Thou art a superstitious fool.
Prepare us instantly for our departure.   315
Past sorrows, let us moderately lament them,
For those to come, seek wisely to prevent them.

Exeunt [DUCHESS *and* CARIOLA]

299–305 According to 172 above, Antonio was to go directly to Ancona and by now
       might be supposed to be on the way, but when she changes the plan the Duchess
       does not refer to Antonio; nevertheless in III.iv.6 s.d. Antonio is with her at
       Loretto. Either this is an error by Webster or we are tacitly to assume that
       Antonio came from Ancona to meet her.
308 *usual train* The number of attendants was a sign of power and prestige:
       Shakespeare's King Lear requires a hundred knights.
311 *the Spa* In Belgium, a famous watering-place; Webster could have found in
       Montaigne, *Essayes*, II.xv, p. 357, adjacent references to Ancona, Lucca, Loretto
       and Spa.

BOSOLA
  A politician is the devil's quilted anvil,
  He fashions all sins on him and the blows
  Are never heard – he may work in a lady's chamber,   320
  As here for proof. What rests, but I reveal
  All to my lord? Oh, this base quality
  Of intelligencer! Why, every quality i'th'world
  Prefers but gain or commendation:
  Now for this act I am certain to be raised,   325
  And men that paint weeds – to the life – are praised. *Exit*

[Act III,] Scene iii

[*Enter* CARDINAL, FERDINAND, MALATESTE, PESCARA,
SILVIO, *and* DELIO]

CARDINAL
  Must we turn soldier then?
MALATESTE   The Emperor
  Hearing your worth that way, ere you attained
  This reverend garment, joins you in commission
  With the right fortunate soldier, the Marquis of Pescara,
  And the famous Lannoy.
CARDINAL   He that had the honour   5
  Of taking the French King prisoner?
MALATESTE   The same.
  [*Shows plan*] Here's a plot drawn for a new fortification,
  At Naples.
FERDINAND This great Count Malateste I perceive
  Hath got employment?
DELIO   No employment, my lord,   10
  A marginal note in the muster-book that he is
  A voluntary lord.
FERDINAND   He's no soldier?

---

324 *Prefers* Assists in bringing about (*OED*)

  0 s.d. ed. (SCENA III. / *Cardinall, Ferdinand, Mallateste, Pescara, Siluio, Delio, Bosola.* Q1)
  1 *Emperor* Charles V
  3 *reverend garment* the robes of a cardinal
  5 *famous Lannoy* The historical figure Charles de Lannoy (c.1487-1527) received the surrendered sword of Francis I of France at the battle of Pavia in 1525.
  7 *plot* ground-plan
12–13 ed. (one line Q1)

DELIO

   He has worn gunpowder in's hollow tooth,
   For the tooth-ache.

SILVIO

   He comes to the leaguer with a full intent
   To eat fresh beef and garlic, means to stay   15
   Till the scent be gone, and straight return to court.

DELIO

   He hath read all the late service,
   As the city chronicle relates it,
   And keeps two painters going, only to express
   Battles in model.

SILVIO   Then he'll fight by the book.   20

DELIO

   By the almanac, I think,
   To choose good days and shun the critical. –
   That's his mistress' scarf.

SILVIO   Yes, he protests
   He would do much for that taffeta.

DELIO

   I think he would run away from a battle   25
   To save it from taking prisoner.

SILVIO   He is horribly afraid
   Gunpowder will spoil the perfume on't.

DELIO

   I saw a Dutchman break his pate once
   For calling him pot-gun: he made his head
   Have a bore in't like a musket.   30

SILVIO

   I would he had made a touch-hole to't.

---

14 *leaguer* army camp

17 *service* military campaign

19 *keeps* ed. (keepe Q1)

   painters Q1c (Pewterers Q1a-b)

20 *model* drawings made to scale

   by the book only theoretically. The phrase means 'strictly according to the rules', whether in a good sense or bad – see *Romeo and Juliet*, I.v.110, III.i.102.

29 *pot-gun* child's toy pop-gun, hence braggart

31 *touch-hole* hole in the breech for igniting the charge

[DELIO]

He is indeed a guarded sumpter-cloth
Only for the remove of the court.

> [*Enter* BOSOLA, *who speaks apart to* FERDINAND *and
> the* CARDINAL]

PESCARA

Bosola arriv'd? What should be the business?
Some falling-out amongst the cardinals.   35
These factions amongst great men, they are like
Foxes: when their heads are divided
They carry fire in their tails, and all the country
About them goes to wrack for it.

SILVIO   What's that Bosola?

DELIO

I knew him in Padua, a fantastical scholar, like such who   40
study to know how many knots was in Hercules' club, of
what colour Achilles' beard was, or whether Hector were
not troubled with the tooth-ache. He hath studied himself
half blear-eyed to know the true symmetry of Caesar's nose
by a shoeing-horn, and this he did to gain the name of a   45
speculative man.

PESCARA

Mark Prince Ferdinand,
A very salamander lives in's eye
To mock the eager violence of fire.

SILVIO

That Cardinal hath made more bad faces with his   50
oppression than ever Michael Angelo made good ones; he
lifts up's nose like a foul porpoise before a storm.

---

32 *DELIO He* ed. (He Q1) The catchword at the bottom of the preceding page,
    G4v, is *Del*. NCW suggest the omission of the s.p. occurred because the com-
    positor went from G4v to the inner forme of H (H1v and H2r) before returning
    to H1r, when he overlooked it.
    guarded sumpter-cloth ornamented cloth covering a pack-horse or mule
37–8 Alluding to Judges 15.4 and the trick of Samson who tied pairs of foxes
    together by their tails, attached firebrands to them, and sent them into the
    Philistines' crops to destroy them.
40–6 ed. (as verse Q1)
48 *salamander* supposed to live in fire, the element of passion, destruction or tor-
    ment.
51–2 ed. (as verse Q1)
52 *porpoise* (por-pisse Q1)

PESCARA
  The Lord Ferdinand laughs.
DELIO   Like a deadly cannon
  That lightens ere it smokes.
PESCARA
  These are your true pangs of death,   55
  The pangs of life that struggle with great statesmen.
DELIO
  In such a deformed silence witches whisper their charms.
CARDINAL
  Doth she make religion her riding-hood
  To keep her from the sun, and tempest?
FERDINAND   That –
  That damns her: Methinks her fault and beauty,   60
  Blended together, show like leprosy,
  The whiter, the fouler: I make it a question
  Whether her beggarly brats were ever christened.
CARDINAL
  I will instantly solicit the state of Ancona
  To have them banished.
FERDINAND   You are for Loretto?   65
  I shall not be at your ceremony: fare you well.
  [*To* BOSOLA] Write to the Duke of Malfi, my young nephew
  She had by her first husband, and acquaint him
  With's mother's honesty.
BOSOLA   I will.
FERDINAND   Antonio?
  A slave that only smelled of ink and counters,   70
  And ne'er in's life looked like a gentleman
  But in the audit time! Go, go presently,
  Draw me out an hundred and fifty of our horse,
  And meet me at the fort bridge.

                                           Exeunt

59–61 ed. (That ... and / Beauty ... leaprosie Q1)

67–9 This is the only reference to this son. Perhaps he is a 'ghost character' from an
    early draft whom Webster forgot to delete. His existence seems incompatible
    with Ferdinand's hope at IV.ii.273 of inheriting a mass of treasure at the
    Duchess' death.

70 *counters* small discs used in accounting

71 *life* ed. (like Q1)

73 *hundred* ed. (hundreth Q1)

[Act III,] Scene iv

[Enter] TWO PILGRIMS *to the shrine of Our Lady of*
Loretto

1 PILGRIM
I have not seen a goodlier shrine than this,
Yet I have visited many.
2 PILGRIM   The Cardinal of Aragon
Is this day to resign his cardinal's hat,
His sister Duchess likewise is arrived
To pay her vow of pilgrimage. I expect   5
A noble ceremony.
1 PILGRIM   No question. – They come.

> *Here the ceremony of the Cardinal's instalment in the*
> *habit of a soldier: performed in delivering up his cross,*
> *hat, robes and ring, at the shrine; and investing him*
> *with sword, helmet, shield, and spurs: then* ANTONIO,
> *the* DUCHESS *and their children, having presented*
> *themselves at the shrine, are by a form of banishment*
> *in dumb-show, expressed towards them by the*
> CARDINAL *and the State of Ancona, banished; during*
> *all which ceremony, this ditty is sung to very solemn*
> *music, by divers churchmen; and then*

> *Exeunt.*

0 s.d. ed. (SCENA IIII. / *Two Pilgrimes to the Shrine of our Lady of* Loretto. Q1).
   The traditional dress of a pilgrim consisted of a gown, staff, scallop-shell, scrip and
   bottle, as described in Sir Walter Raleigh's poem 'The passionate man's Pilgrimage'.
   shrine The actual Loretto shrine featured a black madonna with child, and
   Webster may have intended an elaborate imitation, a spectacle composing a pattern with the later spectacular staging of the bodies (IV.i) and the tomb (V.iii).
   See Introduction p. xxxix–l.
6 s.d. 2 *habit* Q1b (*order* Q1a): *of a* ed. (*a* Q1)
6 s.d. 5 *children* A boy, a girl old enough to say her prayers (see IV.ii.194–6) and
   a babe in arms.
6 s.d. 7 *in dumb-show* Q1b (not in Q1a). This dumb-show must include the violent removal of the wedding-ring from the finger of the Duchess, as lines 35–6
   indicate. The dumb-show signals a decisive turning point with the Cardinal's
   transformation into soldier and the simultaneous subjection suffered by the
   Duchess. The presence of Antonio seems to contradict III.ii.172 where the
   Duchess tells him to go to Ancona. See above, III.ii.299–305n.
6 s.d. 9 *ditty* Q1b (*Hymne* Q1a)

Arms, and honours, deck thy story
To thy fame's eternal glory,
Adverse fortune ever fly thee,
No disastrous fate come nigh thee.   The author   10
                                                        disclaims
I alone will sing thy praises,   this ditty
Whom to honour, virtue raises;   to be his
And thy study, that divine is,
Bent to martial discipline is.
Lay aside all those robes lie by thee,   15
Crown thy arts with arms: they'll beautify thee.

Oh worthy of worthiest name, adorned in this manner,
Lead bravely thy forces on, under war's warlike banner:
Oh mayest thou prove fortunate in all martial courses,
Guide thou still, by skill, in arts and forces: 20
Victory attend thee nigh whilst fame sings loud thy powers,
Triumphant conquest crown thy head, and blessings pour
   down showers.

1 PILGRIM
   Here's a strange turn of state: who would have thought
   So great a lady would have matched herself
   Unto so mean a person? Yet the Cardinal   25
   Bears himself much too cruel.
2 PILGRIM   They are banished.
1 PILGRIM
   But I would ask what power hath this state
   Of Ancona to determine of a free prince?
2 PILGRIM
   They are a free state sir, and her brother showed
   How that the Pope, forehearing of her looseness,   30
   Hath seized into the protection of the Church
   The dukedom which she held as dowager.

---

7 *Arms* Q1b (The Hymne. / *Armes* Q1a) (but the catch-word in Q1b is not corrected and reads 'The')

10–13 *The ... his* Q1b (opposite line 3 on sig H2r – not in Q1a). Presumably added
   by Webster when he read the text in proof. The author of the ditty has not been
   identified.

19 *courses* encounters

29 *free state* Ancona had been an independent republic but by Webster's time was
   one of the Papal States, and as 2 Pilgrim explains, this gives the Cardinal an
   excuse to act ostensibly in the name of the Papacy to gain his revenge.
   state sir Q1b (state Q1a)

31 *Hath* Q1b (Had Q1a)

1 PILGRIM
  But by what justice?
2 PILGRIM   Sure I think by none,
  Only her brother's instigation.
1 PILGRIM
  What was it with such violence he took   35
  Off from her finger?
2 PILGRIM   'Twas her wedding ring,
  Which he vowed shortly he would sacrifice
  To his revenge.
1 PILGRIM   Alas, Antonio,
  If that a man be thrust into a well,
  No matter who sets hand to't, his own weight   40
  Will bring him sooner to th'bottom. Come, let's hence.
  Fortune makes this conclusion general,
  'All things do help th'unhappy man to fall'.

Exeunt

[Act III,] Scene v

[*Enter* ANTONIO, DUCHESS, CHILDREN, CARIOLA, *and*
SERVANTS]

DUCHESS
  Banished Ancona?
ANTONIO   Yes, you see what power
  Lightens in great men's breath.
DUCHESS   Is all our train
  Shrunk to this poor remainder?
ANTONIO   These poor men,
  Which have got little in your service, vow
  To take your fortune; but your wiser buntings,   5
  Now they are fledged, are gone.

---

36 *Off* ed. (Of Q1)

  0 s.d. ed. (SCENA V. / *Antonio, Duchesse, Children, Cariola, Seruants, Bosola,
    Souldiers, with Vizards.* Q1)
    As line 82 indicates, Cariola has the baby in her arms.
  2 *Lightens* An intransitive verb, 'flashes like lightning' – as at III.iii.54.
  5 *buntings* small birds related to the lark but without their song: here applied to
    the servants who have had the wit to see that it is time to leave and the means to
    do so.

DUCHESS   They have done wisely.
  This puts me in mind of death: physicians thus,
  With their hands full of money, use to give o'er
  Their patients.
ANTONIO   Right the fashion of the world:
  From decayed fortunes every flatterer shrinks,   10
  Men cease to build where the foundation sinks.
DUCHESS
  I had a very strange dream tonight.
ANTONIO   What was't?
DUCHESS
  Methought I wore my coronet of state,
  And on a sudden all the diamonds
  Were changed to pearls.
ANTONIO   My interpretation   15
  Is, you'll weep shortly, for to me the pearls
  Do signify your tears.
DUCHESS   The birds that live i'th'field
  On the wild benefit of nature, live
  Happier than we; for they may choose their mates
  And carol their sweet pleasures to the spring.   20

     [*Enter* BOSOLA *with a letter which he presents to the*
                  DUCHESS]

BOSOLA
  You are happily o'er-ta'en.
DUCHESS   From my brother?
BOSOLA
  Yes, from the Lord Ferdinand your brother,
  All love, and safety.
DUCHESS   Thou dost blanch mischief,
  Wouldst make it white. See, see, like to calm weather
  At sea before a tempest, false hearts speak fair   25
  To those they intend most mischief.
  [*Reads*] *Send Antonio to me, I want his head in a*
    business –
  A politic equivocation:
  He doth not want your counsel but your head: 30
  That is, he cannot sleep till you be dead;
  And here's another pitfall that's strewed o'er
  With roses: mark it, 'tis a cunning one:

  9 *Right* Just
 18 *benefit* gift
 27–9 ed. (one line Q1)

[*Reads*] *I stand engaged for your husband, for several*
    debts, at Naples; let not that trouble him, I had rather   35
    have his heart than his money.
And I believe so too.
BOSOLA   What do you believe?
DUCHESS
    That he so much distrusts my husband's love
    He will by no means believe his heart is with him
    Until he see it. The devil is not cunning enough   40
    To circumvent us in riddles.
BOSOLA
    Will you reject that noble and free league
    Of amity and love which I present you?
DUCHESS
    Their league is like that of some politic kings
    Only to make themselves of strength and power   45
    To be our after-ruin: tell them so.
BOSOLA
    And what from you?
ANTONIO   Thus tell him: I will not come.
BOSOLA
    And what of this?
ANTONIO   My brothers have dispersed
    Bloodhounds abroad; which till I hear are muzzled,
    No truce, though hatched with ne'er such politic skill,   50
    Is safe, that hangs upon our enemies' will.
    I'll not come at them.
BOSOLA   This proclaims your breeding.
    Every small thing draws a base mind to fear
    As the adamant draws iron. Fare you well sir,
    You shall shortly hear from's.   *Exit*
DUCHESS   I suspect some ambush: 55
    Therefore by all my love I do conjure you
    To take your eldest son and fly towards Milan;
    Let us not venture all this poor remainder
    In one unlucky bottom.

34–6 ed. (as verse Q1)
        This was the (invented) reason the Duchess gave for dismissing Antonio at
        III.ii.164–8. Presumably Bosola, who was present then, reported it like a dutiful
        spy.
48 *brothers* i.e. brothers-in-law
54 *adamant* magnet
58–9 *venture ... bottom* Alluding to the proverb, 'Venture not all in one bottom',
        do not risk all your wealth in one ship.

ANTONIO   You counsel safely:
  Best of my life, farewell; since we must part   60
  Heaven hath a hand in't; but no other wise
  Than as some curious artist takes in sunder
  A clock, or watch, when it is out of frame,
  To bring't in better order.
DUCHESS   I know not which is best,
  To see you dead, or part with you: farewell boy,   65
  Thou art happy that thou hast not understanding
  To know thy misery; for all our wit
  And reading brings us to a truer sense
  Of sorrow. In the eternal Church, sir,
  I do hope we shall not part thus.
ANTONIO   Oh, be of comfort.   70
  Make patience a noble fortitude,
  And think not how unkindly we are used:
  'Man, like to cassia, is proved best, being bruised'.
DUCHESS
  Must I like to a slave-born Russian
  Account it praise to suffer tyranny?   75
  And yet, oh heaven, thy heavy hand is in't.
  I have seen my little boy oft scourge his top
  And compared myself to't: nought made me e'er
  Go right but heaven's scourge-stick.
ANTONIO   Do not weep:
  Heaven fashioned us of nothing; and we strive   80
  To bring ourselves to nothing. Farewell Cariola

---

65 *boy* Addressing her son.

69 *the eternal Church* the congregation of the saved in Heaven. The phrase occurs
    in Sidney, *Arcadia* (*Works* I. 233), one of a small cluster of borrowings at this
    point by Webster from Sidney.

73 '*Man* Q1b (Man Q1a); *bruised*' ed. (bruiz'd Q1a, Q1b)

74–5 From Sidney, *Astrophil and Stella*, Sonnet 2: 'and now like slave-borne
    Muscovite / I call it praise to suffer Tyrannie'. *Astrophil and Stella* was included
    with the *Arcadia* in editions from 1598 on (see *The Poems of Sir Philip Sidney*,
    ed. William A. Ringler Jr. (Oxford 1962), p. lxii.

77–8 Compare Sidney, *Arcadia* (*Works* I. 227): 'Griefe onely makes his wretched
    state to see / (Even like a toppe which nought but whipping moves)'.

78–9 ed. (And ... right, / But ... sticke / Q1)

79 *scourge-stick* whip used to make a child's top spin

80–1 From Donne, *An Anatomy of the World*, lines 155–7, but Donne's 'God' has
    been altered to 'Heaven'. See the Note on the Text for a discussion of this cen-
    sorship.

And thy sweet armful. – [*To* DUCHESS] If I do never see thee
  more,
Be a good mother to your little ones,
And save them from the tiger. Fare you well.

DUCHESS
Let me look upon you once more: for that speech   85
Came from a dying father. Your kiss is colder
Than that I have seen an holy anchorite
Give to a dead man's skull.

ANTONIO
My heart is turned to a heavy lump of lead,
With which I sound my danger: fare you well.   90

                    Exit [*with his eldest son*]

DUCHESS
My laurel is all withered.

CARIOLA
Look, madam, what a troop of armed men
Make toward us.

      [*Enter* BOSOLA *with a guard with vizards*]

DUCHESS   Oh they are very welcome:
When Fortune's wheel is overcharged with princes
The weight makes it move swift. I would have my ruin   95
Be sudden. [*To* BOSOLA] I am your adventure, am I not?

BOSOLA
You are. You must see your husband no more.

DUCHESS
What devil art thou that counterfeits heaven's thunder?

---

82 *sweet armful* The Duchess' youngest child
     never see thee more The phrase is an echo of III.ii.140 and recurs at IV.i.24 and
     V.iii.41.
87 *anchorite* hermit
89–90 As the depth of water is gauged (*sounded*) with a lead-weighted line, so the
     weight of Antonio's heavy heart can sound the danger.
91 An ominous sign, referred to in Shakespeare, *Richard II*, II.iv.7–8.
93 s.d. The use of masks by the soldiers, and Bosola, is menacing. The play contains
     many textual references to disguise and masks, reinforced in visual terms by this
     episode, by the stage presentation of a masque of madmen, and Bosola's various
     disguises.
95 *move* Q1b (more Q1a)
96 *I … adventure* I am your target (but possibly in an ironic sense, 'You aim to find
     me as if by chance').

BOSOLA

    Is that terrible? I would have you tell me

    Whether is that note worse that frights the silly birds   100

    Out of the corn, or that which doth allure them

    To the nets? You have harkened to the last too much. *caught*

DUCHESS

    Oh misery: like to a rusty o'er-charged cannon,

    Shall I never fly in pieces? Come: to what prison?

BOSOLA

    To none.

DUCHESS   Whither then?

BOSOLA   To your palace.   105

DUCHESS

    I have heard that Charon's boat serves to convey

    All o'er the dismal lake, but brings none back again.

BOSOLA

    Your brothers mean you safety and pity.

DUCHESS   Pity?

    With such a pity men preserve alive

    Pheasants and quails, when they are not fat enough   110

    To be eaten.

BOSOLA   These are your children?

DUCHESS   Yes.

BOSOLA   Can they prattle?

DUCHESS   No:

    But I intend, since they were born accursed,

    Curses shall be their first language.

BOSOLA   Fie, madam,

    Forget this base, low fellow.

DUCHESS   Were I a man

    I'd beat that counterfeit face into thy other.   115

BOSOLA

    One of no birth.

---

  99 s.p. Q1b (not in Q1a)

100 *silly* weak, defenceless

103 s.p. Q1b (*Ant.* Q1a)

      o'er-charged ed. (ore-char'd Q1)

103–4 The image is used for the soul leaving the body at death by Donne, *Of the Progress of the Soul: The Second Anniversary*, lines 181-2.

106 *Charon's boat* In Classical mythology Charon was the ferryman who conveyed the dead across the river Styx to Hades.

108–9 ed. (Your ... pitie. / Pitie ... aliue. Q1)

115 *counterfeit face* vizard

DUCHESS   Say that he was born mean:
　　Man is most happy when's own actions
　　Be arguments and examples of his virtue.
BOSOLA
　　A barren, beggarly virtue.
DUCHESS
　　I prithee who is greatest, can you tell?   120
　　Sad tales befit my woe: I'll tell you one.
　　A salmon as she swam unto the sea
　　Met with a dog-fish who encounters her
　　With this rough language: 'Why art thou so bold
　　To mix thyself with our high state of floods,   125
　　Being no eminent courtier, but one
　　That for the calmest and fresh time o'th'year
　　Dost live in shallow rivers, rank'st thyself
　　With silly smelts and shrimps? And darest thou
　　Pass by our dog-ship without reverence?'   130
　　'Oh', quoth the salmon, 'sister be at peace:
　　Thank Jupiter we both have passed the net,
　　Our value never can be truly known
　　Till in the fisher's basket we be shown.
　　I'th'market then my price may be the higher   135
　　Even when I am nearest to the cook, and fire'.
　　So to great men the moral may be stretched:
　　'Men oft are valued high, when th'are most wretched'.
　　But come, whither you please: I am armed 'gainst misery,
　　Bent to all sways of the oppressor's will.   140
　　'There's no deep valley, but near some great hill'.

　　　　　　　　　　　　　　　　　　　　Exeunt

Act IV, Scene i

[*Enter* FERDINAND, BOSOLA, *and* SERVANTS *with torches*]

FERDINAND
　　How doth our sister Duchess bear herself
　　In her imprisonment?

0 s.d. ed. (ACTVS IIII. SCENA. I. / *Ferdinand, Bosola, Dutchesse, Cariola, Seruants.* Q1)
　　Torches and candles, brought on stage, would indicate that this is a night-scene (see lines 24–6).
2 *imprisonment* This presumably means (for the moment at least) house-arrest, since in III.v.105 Bosola tells the Duchess she is to be taken to her palace not

BOSOLA   Nobly, I'll describe her:
  She's sad, as one long used to't, and she seems
  Rather to welcome the end of misery
  Than shun it: a behaviour so noble   5
  As gives a majesty to adversity:
  You may discern the shape of loveliness
  More perfect in her tears than in her smiles;
  She will muse four hours together, and her silence,
  Methinks, expresseth more than if she spake.   10
FERDINAND
  Her melancholy seems to be fortified
  With a strange disdain.
BOSOLA   'Tis so: and this restraint,
  Like English mastiffs that grow fierce with tying,
  Makes her too passionately apprehend
  Those pleasures she's kept from.
FERDINAND   Curse upon her: 15
  I will no longer study in the book
  Of another's heart: inform her what I told you.   *Exit*

                [*Enter* DUCHESS *and* CARIOLA]

BOSOLA
  All comfort to your grace.
DUCHESS   I will have none:
  Pray thee, why dost thou wrap thy poisoned pills
  In gold and sugar?   20

---

some prison; but she may be imagined as moved to a dungeon for her killing (see
IV.ii.11 and n.). There is a general parallel between the fate of the Duchess and
the royal figures of Marlowe's Edward II and of Richard II in Shakespeare,
except that Webster's Duchess is brought not at once but by progressive degrees
to mortification: here she is still dressed with the dignity proper to her rank, but
Bosola proposes (115ff.) that she is to wear a penitential garment next her skin
and have beads and a prayer-book, and this may indicate how she is to appear
in the next scene – her last – IV.ii.

3–5 From Sidney, *Arcadia* (*Works* I. 332).

5–6 Taken from Sidney, *Arcadia* (*Works* I. 16): 'a behaviour so noble, as gave a
     majestie to adversitie'.

7–8 The cadence is close to Sidney, *Arcadia* (*Works* I. 333): 'perceyve the shape of
     lovelinesse more perfectly in wo, then in joyfulnesse' – and Webster's words also
     recall *King Lear*, IV.iii.16–22.

9 *four hours* A common expression for 'several hours' as in *Hamlet*, 2.2.160.

12–15 From Sidney, *Arcadia* (*Works* I. 25).

BOSOLA
   Your elder brother the Lord Ferdinand
   Is come to visit you, and sends you word,
   'Cause once he rashly made a solemn vow
   Never to see you more, he comes i'th'night:
   And prays you, gently, neither torch nor taper   25
   Shine in your chamber. He will kiss your hand
   And reconcile himself, but, for his vow,
   He dares not see you.
DUCHESS   At his pleasure:
   Take hence the lights.

                  [*Exeunt* SERVANTS *with torches*]

                  [*Enter* FERDINAND]

                  He's come.
FERDINAND
   Where are you?
DUCHESS   Here, sir.
FERDINAND   This darkness suits you well.   30
DUCHESS
   I would ask you pardon.
FERDINAND   You have it;
   For I account it the honorabl'st revenge,
   Where I may kill, to pardon. Where are your cubs?
DUCHESS
   Whom?
FERDINAND Call them your children;
   For though our national law distinguish bastards   35
   From true legitimate issue, compassionate nature
   Makes them all equal.
DUCHESS   Do you visit me for this?
   You violate a sacrament o'th'Church
   Shall make you howl in hell for't.
FERDINAND   It had been well
   Could you have lived thus always, for indeed   40
   You were too much i'th'light. But no more.
   I come to seal my peace with you. Here's a hand

---

21 *elder brother* Since in IV.ii.257 Ferdinand declares he is her twin, here presumably Bosola must be supposed mistaken, or to mean that Ferdinand was the first
   twin to be born, or Webster is being careless.
24 *i'th'night* Conventionally indicated on the Elizabethan stage by the bringing on
   of torches or candles. See Introduction p. xxxviii.
33 *cubs* The first touch of the Duke's future lycanthropia? (Lucas)
41 *i'th'light* in the public eye (and with a play upon *light* = wanton)

To which you have vowed much love: the ring upon't
You gave.

Gives her a dead man's hand

DUCHESS   I affectionately kiss it.
FERDINAND
Pray do, and bury the print of it in your heart.   45
I will leave this ring with you for a love token,
And the hand, as sure as the ring; and do not doubt
But you shall have the heart too. When you need a friend
Send it to him that owned it: you shall see
Whether he can aid you.
DUCHESS   You are very cold.   50
I fear you are not well after your travel –
Ha? Lights! – Oh horrible!
FERDINAND   Let her have lights enough. *Exit*

[*Enter* SERVANTS *with torches*]

DUCHESS
What witchcraft doth he practise, that he hath left
A dead man's hand here?

*Here is discovered behind a traverse the artificial
figures of* ANTONIO *and his children, appearing as if
they were dead.*

BOSOLA
Look you, here's the piece from which 'twas ta'en.   55

---

43 *the ring upon't* Recalling I.i.407 when the Duchess put a ring on Antonio's
finger. In most productions until the twentieth century the dead man's hand was
not used – in 1850 it was Ferdinand's own 'cold hand' which was kissed. In the
1980 production the Duchess threw the horribly realistic hand into the audience.
(PinP, p. 151).

44 It is so dark the Duchess assumes it is Ferdinand's own hand. Her concerned
reaction that he feels cold shows by the starkest contrast how cruel and perverse
he has become. M. C. Bradbrook, *MLR* (1947), pp. 283–94, points out that,
ironically, a dead man's hand was a charm supposed to cure madness.

54 s.d. *traverse* A curtain drawn back to discover the tableau. This spectacle of the
dead bodies of Antonio and the children is the severest test of the Duchess' sanity
and faith. Fifty-five lines later, Webster allows the audience (but not the
Duchess) to learn that these figures were waxwork not real. In Jacobean performances they could, as in *The Winter's Tale*, have been represented by real
actors and this would have been the simplest method, the audience taking their
cue from the Duchess and accepting the figures as dead. Webster makes a point
about the deceptive illusionism of theatre: the identical theatrical sign can be
treacherously unstable, can be interpreted in opposite ways.

He doth present you this sad spectacle,
That now you know directly they are dead.
Hereafter you may, wisely, cease to grieve
For that which cannot be recovered.

DUCHESS

There is not between heaven and earth one wish   60
I stay for after this: it wastes me more
Than were't my picture, fashioned out of wax,
Stuck with a magical needle, and then buried
In some foul dung-hill; and yond's an excellent property
For a tyrant, which I would account mercy.

BOSOLA   What's that?   65

DUCHESS

If they would bind me to that lifeless trunk
And let me freeze to death.

BOSOLA   Come, you must live.

DUCHESS

That's the greatest torture souls feel in hell,
In hell: that they must live, and cannot die.
Portia, I'll new kindle thy coals again   70
And revive the rare and almost dead example
Of a loving wife.

BOSOLA   Oh fie: despair? Remember
You are a Christian.

DUCHESS   The Church enjoins fasting:
I'll starve myself to death.

BOSOLA   Leave this vain sorrow.
Things being at the worst, begin to mend: 75
The bee, when he hath shot his sting into your hand,
May then play with your eye-lid.

DUCHESS   Good comfortable fellow,
Persuade a wretch that's broke upon the wheel
To have all his bones new set: entreat him live,
To be executed again. Who must dispatch me?   80
I account this world a tedious theatre,
For I do play a part in't 'gainst my will.

BOSOLA

Come, be of comfort, I will save your life.

---

66 In emblem books the image of a live person bound to a corpse symbolised ill-
   matched marriages, but the Duchess characteristically defies commonplace attitudes, outfacing horror with her love for her husband: perhaps she moves
   towards the corpse and is restrained by Bosola.

70 *Portia* Brutus' wife, who choked herself by putting live coals in her mouth after
   hearing of her husband's defeat and death at Philippi.

81–2 From Sidney, *Arcadia* (*Works* I. 333).

DUCHESS
  Indeed I have not leisure to tend so small a business.
BOSOLA
  Now, by my life, I pity you.
DUCHESS   Thou art a fool then,   85
  To waste thy pity on a thing so wretch'd
  As cannot pity itself. I am full of daggers –
  Puff – let me blow these vipers from me.
  [*To a* SERVANT] What are you?
SERVANT   One that wishes you long life.
DUCHESS
  I would thou wert hanged for the horrible curse   90
  Thou hast given me! I shall shortly grow one
  Of the miracles of pity. I'll go pray – no,
  I'll go curse.
BOSOLA   Oh fie.
DUCHESS   I could curse the stars.
BOSOLA   Oh fearful!
DUCHESS
  And those three smiling seasons of the year
  Into a Russian winter, nay the world   95
  To its first chaos.
BOSOLA
  Look you, the stars shine still.
DUCHESS   Oh, but you must
  Remember, my curse hath a great way to go.
  Plagues, that make lanes through largest families,
  Consume them.
BOSOLA   Fie, lady:
DUCHESS   Let them like tyrants   100
  Never be remembered but for the ill they have done:
  Let all the zealous prayers of mortified
  Churchmen forget them.
BOSOLA   Oh uncharitable.
DUCHESS
  Let heaven a little while cease crowning martyrs

---

87 *itself* ed. (it Q1)
88 *let ... me* let me blow away these poisonous thoughts. The pressure of emotion
    transforms the Duchess' metaphor as she speaks: the daggers become the stings
    of snakes (a supplementary image of stinging pain) which she would blow off (as
    if they were burrs).
    vipers Q1 (vapours Brown). Brown supposes the scribe misread ms 'vapors'.
89–91 *What ... me* From Sidney, *Arcadia* (*Works* I. 485).
99 *make lanes* As does a cannon-ball through a formation of troops in battle.
100 *them* the brothers

To punish them.   105
Go howl them this and say I long to bleed:
'It is some mercy, when men kill with speed'.

                              Exeunt [DUCHESS *and* CARIOLA]

                         [*Enter* FERDINAND]

FERDINAND
  Excellent, as I would wish, she's plagued in art.
  These presentations are but framed in wax
  By the curious master in that quality,   110
  Vincentio Lauriola, and she takes them
  For true substantial bodies.
BOSOLA   Why do you do this?
FERDINAND
  To bring her to despair.
BOSOLA   Faith, end here
  And go no farther in your cruelty.
  Send her a penitential garment to put on   115
  Next to her delicate skin, and furnish her
  With beads and prayer books.
FERDINAND   Damn her, that body of hers,
  While that my blood ran pure in't, was more worth
  Than that which thou wouldst comfort, called a soul.
  I will send her masques of common courtesans,   120
  Have her meat served up by bawds and ruffians,
  And, 'cause she'll needs be mad, I am resolved
  To remove forth the common hospital
  All the mad-folk and place them near her lodging;
  There let them practise together, sing and dance   125
  And act their gambols to the full o'th'moon.
  If she can sleep the better for it, let her.
  Your work is almost ended.
BOSOLA
  Must I see her again?
FERDINAND   Yes.
BOSOLA   Never.
FERDINAND   You must.
BOSOLA
  Never in mine own shape,   130
  That's forfeited by my intelligence

---

108 Ferdinand has evidently watched and heard everything from concealment, a soli-
     tary voyeur.
110 *curious* ingenious
115–17 See below, note to IV.ii.0 s.d.
131 *intelligence* spying

And this last cruel lie. When you send me next
The business shall be comfort.
FERDINAND   Very likely,
Thy pity is nothing of kin to thee. Antonio
Lurks about Milan, thou shalt shortly thither   135
To feed a fire as great as my revenge,
Which ne'er will slack till it have spent his fuel:
'Intemperate agues make physicians cruel'.

Exeunt

[Act IV,] Scene ii

[*Enter* DUCHESS *and* CARIOLA]

DUCHESS
What hideous noise was that?
CARIOLA   'Tis the wild consort
Of madmen, lady, which your tyrant brother
Hath placed about your lodging; this tyranny
I think was never practised till this hour.

133 *Very likely* This is said and meant ironically – a small touch by which Webster
     stresses that Ferdinand does not detect the growing crisis in Bosola's personality,
     the split between cynicism and compassion.

  0 s.d. ed. (SCENA II. / *Duchesse, Cariola, Seruant, Mad-men, Bosola,
     Executioners, Ferdinand.* Q1)
     The Duchess may be dressed as a penitent (see IV.i.115–17). Brennan notes that
     ecclesiastical courts sentenced adulteresses to walk through the streets in a pen-
     itential garment of white, with hair unbound and carrying a lighted taper. Jane
     Shore appears thus in Heywood's play of 1599, *The Second Part of King Edward
     the Fourth*. It is not clear whether in line 11 the Duchess is saying that she finds
     her loss of liberty generally depressing, or that she has been moved to an actual
     prison – which would be something very ominous, a suitable place for a killing,
     as in Marlowe's *Edward II* and Shakespeare's *Richard II*. In Webster's time such
     a location would be left to the imagination of the spectators, perhaps aided by
     simple props.
  1 *consort* company – with a play on the sense 'group of musicians' – and there may
     be play on *noise* which also could mean 'group of musicians'. Webster may have
     thus intended to alert his audience to the parodies of a charivari and of a
     Jacobean court wedding masque (see Introduction p. xxx). In a wedding masque
     the anti-masque precisely inverted, in grotesque manner, the harmonies and
     costly elegance of the main masque, in music, words, dance and costume.

DUCHESS
   Indeed I thank him: nothing but noise and folly   5
   Can keep me in my right wits, whereas reason
   And silence make me stark mad. Sit down,
   Discourse to me some dismal tragedy.
CARIOLA
   Oh 'twill increase your melancholy.
DUCHESS   Thou art deceived,
   To hear of greater grief would lessen mine.   10
   This is a prison?
CARIOLA   Yes, but you shall live
   To shake this durance off.
DUCHESS   Thou art a fool,
   The robin redbreast and the nightingale
   Never live long in cages.
CARIOLA   Pray dry your eyes.
   What think you of, madam?
DUCHESS   Of nothing: 15
   When I muse thus, I sleep.
CARIOLA
   Like a madman, with your eyes open?
DUCHESS
   Dost thou think we shall know one another
   In th'other world?
CARIOLA   Yes, out of question.
DUCHESS
   Oh that it were possible we might   20
   But hold some two days conference with the dead,
   From them I should learn somewhat I am sure
   I never shall know here. I'll tell thee a miracle,
   I am not mad yet, to my cause of sorrow.
   Th'heaven o'er my head seems made of molten brass,   25
   The earth of flaming sulphur, yet I am not mad;
   I am acquainted with sad misery
   As the tanned galley-slave is with his oar.
   Necessity makes me suffer constantly,
   And custom makes it easy. Who do I look like now?   30
CARIOLA
   Like to your picture in the gallery,
   A deal of life in show but none in practice;

11 At Blackfriars and the Globe simple props such as chains and fetters could have
   been enough to suggest a prison cell.
25–6 From Deuteronomy 28.15, 23.
31–2 From Sidney, *Arcadia* (*Works* I. 90).

Or rather like some reverend monument
Whose ruins are even pitied.
DUCHESS   Very proper:
And Fortune seems only to have her eye-sight   35
To behold my tragedy. How now,
What noise is that?

[*Enter* SERVANT]

SERVANT   I am come to tell you
Your brother hath intended you some sport:
A great physician, when the Pope was sick
Of a deep melancholy, presented him   40
With several sorts of madmen, which wild object,
Being full of change and sport, forced him to laugh,
And so th'imposthume broke; the self-same cure
The Duke intends on you.
DUCHESS   Let them come in.
SERVANT
There's a mad lawyer, and a secular priest,   45
A doctor that hath forfeited his wits
By jealousy, an astrologian
That in his works said such a day o'th'month
Should be the day of doom, and failing of't,
Ran mad; an English tailor crazed i'th'brain   50
With the study of new fashion, a gentleman usher
Quite beside himself with care to keep in mind
The number of his lady's salutations,
Or how do you, she employed him in each morning;
A farmer too, an excellent knave in grain,   55
Mad 'cause he was hind'red transportation;
And let one broker that's mad loose to these,
You'd think the devil were among them!
DUCHESS
Sit, Cariola. [*To* SERVANT] – Let them loose when you
     please,
For I am chained to endure all your tyranny.   60

33–4 Anticipating the setting of V.iii.

43 *imposthume* abscess

45 *secular priest* One living in the world as contrasted with those who lived in
     monastic seclusion.

55 *knave in grain* incorrigible rogue (and crooked dealer in corn or wheat).

56 *transportation* export. Lucas notes a specific ruling of 1613 forbidding export of
     grain because of its high domestic price and fear of scarcity.

57 *broker* dealer, retailer

[*Enter* MADMEN]

*Here, by a madman, this song is sung to a dismal kind
of music.*

Oh let us howl some heavy note,
   some deadly doggèd howl,
Sounding, as from the threat'ning throat
   of beasts and fatal fowl.
As ravens, screech-owls, bulls, and bears,   65
   we'll bill and bawl our parts,
Till irksome noise have cloyed your ears
   and corrosived your hearts.
At last whenas our choir wants breath,
   our bodies being blest,   70
We'll sing like swans to welcome death,
   and die in love and rest.

I MADMAN
Doomsday not come yet? I'll draw it nearer by a perspective, or make a glass that shall set all the world on fire upon
an instant. I cannot sleep, my pillow is stuffed with a litter   75
of porcupines.

2 MADMAN
Hell is a mere glass-house, where the devils are continually
blowing up women's souls on hollow irons, and the fire
never goes out.

3 MADMAN
I will lie with every woman in my parish the tenth night: I   80
will tithe them over like hay-cocks.

4 MADMAN
Shall my pothecary out-go me, because I am a cuckold?
I have found out his roguery: he makes allum of his wife's

---

60 s.d. The servant describes eight madmen and Q1 assigns eight to dance, but
allots the song only to one and speeches to four. Only the doctor is characterised
consistently, and the text leaves open the choice, in performance, of the number
of madmen and the way they are dressed.

60 s.d. 2 *song* The music, probably by Robert Johnson, has survived in several mss,
and is in Brown and NCW.

66 *bill* Probably a nonce-word referring to the birds, meaning 'to utter through the
bill or beak'; alternative readings such as *bell* (bellow) or *bawl* are appropriate
to animals not birds.

73–4 *perspective* telescope, magnifying glass

77 *glass-house* There was a glass factory in Blackfriars, and Webster refers to blown
glass, shaped like a pregnant woman's belly, at II.ii.6–10.

82–108 ed. (as verse Q1)

urine, and sells it to Puritans that have sore throats with
over-straining.   theatre gets back @ them   85

1 MADMAN

I have skill in heraldry. - cort of arms

2 MADMAN

Hast?

1 MADMAN

You do give for your crest a woodcock's head, with the
brains picked out on't: you are a very ancient gentleman.

3 MADMAN

Greek is turned Turk, we are only to be saved by the   90
Helvetian translation.

1 MADMAN

Come on sir, I will lay the law to you.

2 MADMAN

O, rather lay a corrosive, the law will eat to the bone.

3 MADMAN

He that drinks but to satisfy nature is damned.

4 MADMAN

If I had my glass here, I would show a sight should make   95
all the women here call me mad doctor.

1 MADMAN

What's he, a rope-maker?

2 MADMAN

No, no, no, a snuffling knave, that while he shows the
tombs will have his hand in a wench's placket.

3 MADMAN

Woe to the caroche that brought home my wife from the   100
masque at three o'clock in the morning, it had a large
feather-bed in it.

---

88 *woodcock's* This bird was proverbially stupid and easy to catch.

89 *picked out* removed (and playing on the sense 'embroidered', associated with the
   idea of the heraldic crest)

90 *turned Turk* become an infidel (i.e. the Greek text of the Bible has been used to
   promote false religion).

90–1 The third Madman is apparently a Puritan, and Puritans were a frequent
   object of satire in the theatre of Webster's day: the Helvetian translation of the
   Bible – the Geneva Bible – of 1560, by Coverdale, Knox, and others, was
   strongly Calvinist in tone. It was condemned by King James I in 1603 as 'partial'
   and 'seditious'.

92 *lay the law* (1) expound the law (2) apply the law as a medicine, make a legal
   charge

98 *snuffling* Probably alluding to the nasal whine affected by Puritans.

99 *placket* slit at the top of a skirt

4 MADMAN
I have pared the devil's nails forty times, roasted them in
raven's eggs, and cured agues with them.

3 MADMAN
Get me three hundred milch bats, to make possets to   105
procure sleep.

4 MADMAN
All the college may throw their caps at me, I have made a
soap boiler costive. It was my masterpiece.

*Here the dance consisting of eight madmen, with
music answerable thereunto, after which*

BOSOLA, *like an old man, enters*

DUCHESS
Is he mad too?

SERVANT   Pray question him: I'll leave you.

[*Exeunt* SERVANT *and* MADMEN]

BOSOLA
I am come to make thy tomb.

DUCHESS   Ha, my tomb?   110
Thou speak'st as if I lay upon my death bed
Gasping for breath: do'st thou perceive me sick?

BOSOLA
Yes, and the more dangerously since thy sickness is
insensible.

DUCHESS
Thou art not mad sure; dost know me?   115

BOSOLA
Yes.

DUCHESS
Who am I?

---

105 *possets* drinks of hot milk curdled by spiced wine or ale
107 *throw their caps at me* concede my superiority
108 *soap boiler costive* Diarrhoea was an occupational hazard in soap- making; *cos-*
     tive = constipated.
108 s.d. A parodic inversion of the form and values of the climactic dance in a mar-
     riage masque, which symbolically expressed harmony, unity and order.
108 s.d. 2 *old man* Conventionally symbolic of Time and Death.
113–33 ed. (as verse Q1)
114 *insensible* Montaigne, *Essayes*, II.xxv, p. 397: 'And onely because we perceive
     not to be sicke, makes our recoverie to prove more difficult'.

BOSOLA

Thou art a box of worm-seed, at best, but a salvatory of
green mummy. What's this flesh? A little cruded milk, fantastical puff paste: our bodies are weaker than those paper　120
prisons boys use to keep flies in – more contemptible, since
ours is to preserve earth worms. Didst thou ever see a lark
in a cage? Such is the soul in the body: this world is like her
little turf of grass, and the heaven o'er our heads like her
looking-glass, only gives us a miserable knowledge of the　125
small compass of our prison.

DUCHESS

Am not I thy Duchess?

BOSOLA

Thou art some great woman sure, for riot begins to sit on
thy forehead, clad in grey hairs, twenty years sooner than
on a merry milkmaid's. Thou sleep'st worse than if a mouse　130
should be forced to take up her lodging in a cat's ear; a little
infant that breeds its teeth, should it lie with thee, would
cry out as if thou wert the more unquiet bed-fellow.

DUCHESS

I am Duchess of Malfi still.

BOSOLA

That makes thy sleeps so broken:　　　　　　　　　　135
'Glories, like glow worms, afar off shine bright,
But looked to near, have neither heat nor light'.

DUCHESS

Thou art very plain.

BOSOLA

My trade is to flatter the dead, not the living.
I am a tomb-maker.　　　　　　　　　　　　　　　　140

---

118 *worm-seed* dried flower-heads of the plant were used as a remedy for intestinal
　　worms: and, alluding to the proverbial association of worms with corpses, there
　　is word-play on *seed* = germ, origin.
　　salvatory ointment box
119 *green mummy* medicine from mummified corpses; it was also believed that fresh
　　corpses could yield a medicinal balsam: this may explain *green*, although the
　　colour and its association with mouldy bones has a Websterian gruesomeness all
　　its own.
　　cruded curded. Alluding to Job 10.10.
120–1 It was proverbial that 'the body is the prison of the soul' (Tilley B497).
　　Webster may also be recalling Shakespeare, *King Lear,* V.ii, where Lear, reunited
　　with his beloved daughter but captured, cries 'Come let's away to prison: / We
　　two alone will sing like birds i' th'cage'.
128 *riot* wantonness
136–7 From *The White Devil,* V.i.40–1.

DUCHESS
And thou com'st to make my tomb?
BOSOLA
Yes.
DUCHESS
Let me be a little merry. Of what stuff wilt thou make it?
BOSOLA
Nay, resolve me first, of what fashion?
DUCHESS
Why, do we grow fantastical in our death-bed, do we affect   145
fashion in the grave?
BOSOLA
Most ambitiously: princes' images on their tombs do not lie
as they were wont, seeming to pray up to heaven, but with
their hands under their cheeks as if they died of the tooth-
ache. They are not carved with their eyes fixed upon the   150
stars, but as their minds were wholly bent upon the world
the self-same way they seem to turn their faces.
DUCHESS
Let me know fully therefore the effect
Of this thy dismal preparation,
This talk fit for a charnel.
BOSOLA   Now I shall.   155

      [*Enter* EXECUTIONERS *with*] *a* [*shrouded*] *coffin, cords*
                and a bell

Here is a present from your princely brothers,
And may it arrive welcome, for it brings
Last benefit, last sorrow.
DUCHESS   Let me see it,
I have so much obedience in my blood
I wish it in their veins, to do them good.   160
BOSOLA
This is your last presence chamber.
               [*Reveals the coffin*]
CARIOLA
Oh my sweet lady.
DUCHESS   Peace, it affrights not me.
BOSOLA
I am the common bell-man,

141–52 ed. (as verse Q1)

155 s.d. The coffin is concealed under a pall or cloth.

163 *bell-man* A charity established by the Common Council of the Merchant Tailors
     guild (of which Webster's father was a member) endowed a bell-man at Newgate
     Prison to make a speech outside the cell of condemned men the night before

That usually is sent to condemned persons
The night before they suffer.
DUCHESS   Even now thou said'st   165
Thou wast a tomb-maker.
BOSOLA   'Twas to bring you
By degrees to mortification. Listen:
  Hark now everything is still,
  The screech owl and the whistler shrill
  Call upon our dame, aloud,   170
  And bid her quickly don her shroud.
  Much you had of land and rent,
  Your length in clay's now competent;
  A long war disturbed your mind,
  Here your perfect peace is signed.   175
  Of what is't fools make such vain keeping?
  Sin their conception, their birth, weeping;
  Their life a general mist of error,
  Their death a hideous storm of terror.
  Strew your hair with powders sweet,   180
  Don clean linen, bathe your feet,
  And (the foul fiend more to check)
  A crucifix let bless your neck.
  'Tis now full tide 'tween night and day,
  End your groan and come away.   185
CARIOLA
Hence villains, tyrants, murderers! Alas,
What will you do with my lady? Call for help!
DUCHESS
To whom? To our next neighbours? They are mad folks.

---

execution and another as they were taken to be hanged at Tyburn. Both speeches
(accompanied by the tolling of a hand-bell) were to put them in mind of their
mortality and urge them to save their souls. The bell is still extant, and on view
in St Sepulchre's church – See Forker, pp. 21–4.

167 *mortification* The spiritual process ending in transcendence of one's earthly concerns and appetites (with a play on the sense 'the state of torpor and insensibil-
ity preceding death').

169 *whistler* Referred to as a fatal bird in Spenser, *Faerie Queene*, 2.12.36.

170 This invocation is the very opposite of that in an epithalamion or marriage-song,
which conventionally bade such birds be silent on the wedding night.

173 *competent* appropriate, sufficient

180 The Duchess is to prepare herself for burial in the same manner as a bride – in
epithalamia brides are bid to strew their hair with sweet powders. A further
irony is the echo of the Duchess' words at III.ii.57–9.

BOSOLA
Remove that noise.

[EXECUTIONERS *seize* CARIOLA]

DUCHESS   Farewell Cariola,
In my last will I have not much to give: 190
A many hungry guests have fed upon me.
Thine will be a poor reversion.
CARIOLA
I will die with her.
DUCHESS
I pray thee look thou giv'st my little boy
Some syrup for his cold, and let the girl   195
Say her prayers ere she sleep.

[EXECUTIONERS *force* CARIOLA *off*]

                    Now what you please:
What death?
BOSOLA   Strangling. Here are your executioners.
DUCHESS
I forgive them.
The apoplexy, catarrh, or cough o'th'lungs
Would do as much as they do.   200
BOSOLA
Doth not death fright you?
DUCHESS   Who would be afraid on't,
Knowing to meet such excellent company
In th'other world?
BOSOLA   Yet, methinks,
The manner of your death should much afflict you:
This cord should terrify you?
DUCHESS   Not a whit.   205
What would it pleasure me to have my throat cut
With diamonds, or to be smothered
With cassia, or to be shot to death with pearls?
I know death hath ten thousand several doors
For men to take their exits; and 'tis found   210
They go on such strange geometrical hinges,
You may open them both ways – any way, for heaven' sake,
So I were out of your whispering. Tell my brothers
That I perceive death, now I am well awake,
Best gift is they can give, or I can take.   215

192 *reversion* bequest
201–3 From Montaigne, *Essayes*, I.xxv, p. 75.
209–10 *death ... exits* From Seneca, and proverbial.

I would fain put off my last woman's fault,
I'd not be tedious to you.
EXECUTIONER   We are ready.
DUCHESS
Dispose my breath how please you, but my body
Bestow upon my women: will you?
EXECUTIONER   Yes.
DUCHESS
Pull, and pull strongly, for your able strength   220
Must pull down heaven upon me –
Yet stay, heaven gates are not so highly arched
As princes' palaces: they that enter there
Must go upon their knees. [*Kneels*] Come violent death,
Serve for mandragora, to make me sleep.   225
Go tell my brothers when I am laid out,
They then may feed in quiet.

                They strangle her

BOSOLA
Where's the waiting woman?
Fetch her. Some other strangle the children.

          [EXECUTIONERS *fetch* CARIOLA, *one goes to strangle the*
                              CHILDREN]

Look you, there sleeps your mistress.
CARIOLA   Oh you are damned   230
Perpetually for this! My turn is next,
Is't not so ordered?
BOSOLA   Yes, and I am glad
You are so well prepared for't.
CARIOLA   You are deceived, sir,
I am not prepared for't! I will not die!
I will first come to my answer and know   235
How I have offended.
BOSOLA   Come, dispatch her.
You kept her counsel, now you shall keep ours.
CARIOLA
I will not die, I must not, I am contracted
To a young gentleman!
EXECUTIONER   [*Shows noose*] Here's your wedding ring.
CARIOLA
Let me but speak with the Duke: I'll discover   240
Treason to his person.
BOSOLA   Delays: throttle her.

---

225 *mandragora* mandrake root, used as a narcotic (see II.v.1).

EXECUTIONER
  She bites and scratches!
CARIOLA   If you kill me now
  I am damned! I have not been at confession
  This two years.
BOSOLA   When.
CARIOLA   I am quick with child.
BOSOLA   Why then,
  Your credit's saved.

                    [*They strangle her*]

                    Bear her into th'next room.   245
  Let this lie still.

          [*Exeunt* EXECUTIONERS *with* CARIOLA'*s body*]

                [*Enter* FERDINAND]

FERDINAND   Is she dead?
BOSOLA   She is what
  You'd have her. But here begin your pity.

      [*Draws the traverse and*] *shows the children strangled*

  Alas, how have these offended?
FERDINAND   The death
  Of young wolves is never to be pitied.
BOSOLA
  Fix your eye here.
FERDINAND   Constantly.
BOSOLA   Do you not weep?   250
  Other sins only speak; murder shrieks out.
  The element of water moistens the earth,
  But blood flies upwards and bedews the heavens.
FERDINAND
  Cover her face. Mine eyes dazzle. She died young.
BOSOLA
  I think not so; her infelicity   255
  Seemed to have years too many.

---

245 *credit* reputation
247 s.d. A grim repetition of the s.d. at IV.i.54.
254 *Mine eyes dazzle* In IV.i the Duchess is associated with light, Ferdinand with
    darkness both spiritual and actual: he insists on visiting her in darkness, and
    later, in V.ii.62 speaks of his cruel sore eyes. See also lines 324–5 below; *dazzle*
    could also refer to the welling up of tears in Ferdinand's eyes – see Martin
    Wiggins, *N&Q* 240, 1995, p. 372.

FERDINAND
    She and I were twins,
    And should I die this instant I had lived
    Her time to a minute.
BOSOLA   It seems she was born first:
    You have bloodily approved the ancient truth   260
    That kindred commonly do worse agree
    Than remote strangers.
FERDINAND   Let me see her face again.
    Why didst not thou pity her? What an excellent
    Honest man might'st thou have been
    If thou hadst borne her to some sanctuary   265
    Or, bold in a good cause, opposed thyself
    With thy advanced sword above thy head
    Between her innocence and my revenge!
    I bade thee, when I was distracted of my wits,
    Go kill my dearest friend, and thou hast done't!   270
    For let me but examine well the cause:
    What was the meanness of her match to me?
    Only, I must confess, I had a hope –
    Had she continued widow – to have gained
    An infinite mass of treasure by her death: 275
    And that was the main cause. Her marriage,
    That drew a stream of gall quite through my heart.
    For thee – as we observe in tragedies
    That a good actor many times is cursed

273–5 This constitutes an important anomaly. At III.iii.67 it is asserted that the
    Duchess has a son by her first marriage. This corresponds to the sources but
    could be a relic of an early draft, a detail Webster accidentally failed to cancel,
    since if it is accepted it means that here Ferdinand – of all people – has somehow
    forgotten about his existence, though Ferdinand is the only person in the play
    (III.iii.67–9) who refers to him: 'the Duke of Malfi, my young nephew'. Brown
    assumes Webster did intend to retain this son by the first marriage of the
    Duchess, and that here Ferdinand is deliberately trying to deceive Bosola or is
    making 'an instinctive attempt to 'cover up' feelings of guilt'. If it is assumed that
    Webster intends there to be this son by the first marriage, then the first child the
    audience know about, the first-born to the Duchess and Antonio, could inherit
    nothing except such personal property as the Duchess is entitled to by her first
    marriage settlement and / or the dower after her first husband's death – scarcely
    an 'infinite mass of treasure'. But the son born in Act II is presented in the clos-
    ing moments of the play as a symbol of hope for the future, so it looks as if
    Webster did intend to cancel the son by the first marriage.
278–95 A close parallel to Shakespeare, *Richard II*, V.vi.30–44, where Bolingbroke
    refuses to reward the murderer of the King.

..ying a villain's part – I hate thee for't;   280
.....for my sake say, thou hast done much ill, well.

....LA

...et me quicken your memory, for I perceive
You are falling into ingratitude: I challenge
The reward due to my service.

FERDINAND   I'll tell thee
What I'll give thee.

BOSOLA   Do.

FERDINAND   I'll give thee a pardon   285
For this murder.

BOSOLA   Ha?

FERDINAND   Yes: and 'tis
The largest bounty I can study to do thee.
By what authority did'st thou execute
This bloody sentence?

BOSOLA   By yours.

FERDINAND   Mine? Was I her judge?
Did any ceremonial form of law   290
Doom her to not-being? Did a complete jury
Deliver her conviction up i'th'court?
Where shalt thou find this judgement registered
Unless in hell? See, like a bloody fool
Th'hast forfeited thy life, and thou shalt die for't.   295

BOSOLA
The office of justice is perverted quite
When one thief hangs another. Who shall dare
To reveal this?

FERDINAND   Oh, I'll tell thee:
The wolf shall find her grave and scrape it up,
Not to devour the corpse but to discover   300
The horrid murder.

BOSOLA   You, not I, shall quake for't.

FERDINAND
Leave me.

BOSOLA   I will first receive my pension.

FERDINAND
You are a villain.

BOSOLA   When your ingratitude
Is judge, I am so.

FERDINAND   O horror,
That not the fear of him which binds the devils   305
Can prescribe man obedience.
Never look upon me more.

299–301 This superstition is referred to in *The White Devil*, V.iv.100–1.

BOSOLA   Why fare thee well.
  Your brother and yourself are worthy men,
  You have a pair of hearts are hollow graves,
  Rotten, and rotting others; and your vengeance,   310
  Like two chained bullets, still goes arm in arm.
  You may be brothers: for treason, like the plague,
  Doth take much in a blood. I stand like one
  That long hath ta'en a sweet and golden dream:
  I am angry with myself now that I wake.   315
FERDINAND
  Get thee into some unknown part o'th'world
  That I may never see thee.
BOSOLA   Let me know
  Wherefore I should be thus neglected. Sir,
  I served your tyranny, and rather strove
  To satisfy yourself than all the world;   320
  And though I loathed the evil yet I loved
  You, that did counsel it, and rather sought
  To appear a true servant than an honest man.
FERDINAND
  I'll go hunt the badger, by owl-light:
  'Tis a deed of darkness.   *Exit*   325
BOSOLA
  He's much distracted. Off, my painted honour;
  While with vain hopes our faculties we tire,
  We seem to sweat in ice, and freeze in fire;
  What would I do, were this to do again?
  I would not change my peace of conscience   330
  For all the wealth of Europe –

                    [DUCHESS *moves*]

                         She stirs! Here's life!
  Return fair soul from darkness, and lead mine
  Out of this sensible hell! She's warm, she breathes:
  Upon thy pale lips I will melt my heart
  To store them with fresh colour. [*Kisses her*] Who's there – 335
  Some cordial drink! – Alas, I dare not call;

---

311 *chained bullets* Cannon-balls linked by chain were used mainly in naval warfare
    to destroy masts and rigging but would also cut swathes through infantry in
    close order.

313 *take ... blood* take hold in certain families

324 *owl-light* dusk

331 s.d. Recalling the momentary revival of Desdemona in *Othello*, V.ii.117–25.

333 *sensible* perceptible, palpable

336 *cordial* invigorating to the heart, reviving

So pity would destroy pity. Her eye opes,
And heaven in it seems to ope, that late was shut,
To take me up to mercy.
DUCHESS   Antonio.
BOSOLA
Yes Madam he is living,   340
The dead bodies you saw were but feigned statues,
He's reconciled to your brothers, the Pope hath wrought
The atonement.
DUCHESS   Mercy.   *She dies*
BOSOLA
Oh, she's gone again: there the cords of life broke.
Oh sacred innocence that sweetly sleeps   345
On turtles' feathers, whilst a guilty conscience
Is a black register wherein is writ
All our good deeds and bad, a perspective
That shows us hell – that we cannot be suffered
To do good when we have a mind to it!   350
This is manly sorrow:
These tears, I am very certain, never grew
In my mother's milk. My estate is sunk
Below the degree of fear: where were
These penitent fountains while she was living?   355
Oh, they were frozen up. Here is a sight
As direful to my soul as is the sword
Unto a wretch hath slain his father.
Come, I'll bear thee hence
And execute thy last will; that's deliver   360
Thy body to the reverend dispose
Of some good women: that the cruel tyrant
Shall not deny me: then I'll post to Milan,
Where somewhat I will speedily enact
Worth my dejection.   365

                    Exit [with the DUCHESS' body]

---

339 *mercy* ed. (merry Q1)
344 *cords of life* heart-strings
348 *perspective* an optical device using mirrors, lenses etc. to produce special or fan-
      tastic effects. The effect of a guilty conscience is to rearrange past deeds, both
      good and bad, into a distorted prospect showing hell.
357–8 ed. (one line Q1)
365 *dejection* dismissal, humiliation

Act V, Scene i

[*Enter* ANTONIO, DELIO]

ANTONIO
What think you of my hope of reconcilement
To the Aragonian brethren?
DELIO   I misdoubt it;
For though they have sent their letters of safe conduct
For your repair to Milan, they appear
But nets to entrap you. The Marquis of Pescara,   5
Under whom you hold certain land in cheat,
Much 'gainst his noble nature hath been moved
To seize those lands, and some of his dependants
Are at this instant making it their suit
To be invested in your revenues.   10
I cannot think they mean well to your life
That do deprive you of your means of life –
Your living.
ANTONIO   You are still an heretic
To any safety I can shape myself.

[*Enter* PESCARA]

DELIO
Here comes the Marquis: I will make myself   15
Petitioner for some part of your land,
To know whether it is flying.
ANTONIO   I pray do.   [*Withdraws*]
DELIO
Sir, I have a suit to you.
PESCARA   To me?
DELIO   An easy one:
There is the citadel of Saint Bennet,
With some demesnes, of late in the possession   20
Of Antonio Bologna; please you bestow them on me?
PESCARA
You are my friend: But this is such a suit
Nor fit for me to give nor you to take.
DELIO
No sir?

---

0 s.d. ed. (ACTVS V. SCENA. I. / *Antonio, Delio, Pescara, Iulia.* Q1)

6 *in cheat* The property would revert to Pescara should Antonio be convicted of
treason or felony (as seems to be the case).

11–13 Recalling *Merchant of Venice*, IV.i.376–7.

[*Enter* JULIA]

PESCARA I will give you ample reason for't
  Soon in private. Here's the Cardinal's mistress.   25
JULIA
  My lord, I am grown your poor petitioner,
  And should be an ill beggar, had I not
  A great man's letter, [*Presents letter*] here, the Cardinal's,
  To court you in my favour.
PESCARA   He entreats for you
  The citadel of Saint Bennet, that belonged   30
  To the banished Bologna.
JULIA   Yes.
PESCARA
  I could not have thought of a friend I could
  Rather pleasure with it: 'tis yours.
JULIA   Sir, I thank you,
  And he shall know how doubly I am engaged
  Both in your gift and speediness of giving,   35
  Which makes your grant the greater.   *Exit*
ANTONIO   [*Aside*] How they fortify
  Themselves with my ruin!
DELIO   Sir, I am
  Little bound to you.
PESCARA   Why?
DELIO
  Because you denied this suit to me, and gave't
  To such a creature.
PESCARA   Do you know what it was?   40
  It was Antonio's land: not forfeited
  By course of law but ravished from his throat
  By the Cardinal's entreaty: it were not fit
  I should bestow so main a piece of wrong
  Upon my friend, 'tis a gratification   45
  Only due to a strumpet, for it is injustice.
  Shall I sprinkle the pure blood of innocents
  To make those followers I call my friends
  Look ruddier upon me? I am glad
  This land, ta'en from the owner by such wrong,   50
  Returns again unto so foul an use
  As salary for his lust. Learn, good Delio,
  To ask noble things of me, and you shall find
  I'll be a noble giver.
DELIO   You instruct me well.
ANTONIO
  [*Aside*] Why, here's a man, now, would fright impudence   55
  From sauciest beggars.

PESCARA   Prince Ferdinand's come to Milan
  Sick, as they give out, of an apoplexy;
  But some say, 'tis a frenzy. I am going
  To visit him.   *Exit*
ANTONIO [*Coming forward*] 'Tis a noble old fellow.
DELIO
  What course do you mean to take, Antonio?   60
ANTONIO
  This night I mean to venture all my fortune
  Which is no more than a poor lingering life
  To the Cardinal's worst of malice. I have got
  Private access to his chamber and intend
  To visit him about the mid of night   65
  As once his brother did our noble Duchess.
  It may be that the sudden apprehension
  Of danger – for I'll go in mine own shape –
  When he shall see it fraught with love and duty,
  May draw the poison out of him, and work   70
  A friendly reconcilement. If it fail,
  Yet it shall rid me of this infamous calling:
  For better fall once than be ever falling.
DELIO
  I'll second you in all danger, and howe'er,
  My life keeps rank with yours.   75
ANTONIO
  You are still my loved and best friend.

                                        Exeunt

[Act V,] Scene ii

[*Enter* PESCARA *and a* DOCTOR]

PESCARA
  Now Doctor, may I visit your patient?
DOCTOR
  If't please your lordship: but he's instantly
  To take the air here in the gallery,
  By my direction.
PESCARA   Pray thee, what's his disease?

58 *frenzy* inflammation of the brain
69 *fraught* ed. (fraight Q1)

0 s.d. ed. (SCENA. II. / *Pescara, a Doctor, Ferdinand, Cardinall, Malateste, Bosola, Iulia.* Q1)

DOCTOR
   A very pestilent disease, my lord,   5
   They call lycanthropia.
PESCARA   What's that?
   I need a dictionary to't.
DOCTOR   I'll tell you:
   In those that are possessed with't there o'er-flows
   Such melancholy humour they imagine
   Themselves to be transformèd into wolves: 10
   Steal forth to church-yards in the dead of night
   And dig dead bodies up: as two nights since
   One met the Duke 'bout midnight in a lane
   Behind St. Mark's church, with the leg of a man
   Upon his shoulder; and he howled fearfully;   15
   Said he was a wolf, only the difference
   Was, a wolf's skin was hairy on the outside,
   His on the inside; bad them take their swords,
   Rip up his flesh, and try. Straight I was sent for,
   And having ministered to him, found his grace   20
   Very well recovered.
PESCARA   I am glad on't.
DOCTOR
   Yet not without some fear of a relapse:
   If he grow to his fit again I'll go
   A nearer way to work with him than ever
   Paracelsus dreamed of: if they'll give me   25
   Leave I'll buffet his madness out of him.
   Stand aside, he comes.

       [*Enter* CARDINAL, FERDINAND, MALATESTE,
          and BOSOLA, *who stays apart*]

FERDINAND
   Leave me.
MALATESTE
   Why doth your lordship love this solitariness?
FERDINAND
   Eagles commonly fly alone: they are crows, daws and star- 30
   lings that flock together. – Look, what's that follows me?

---

  6 *lycanthropia* The name and the details in lines 8–19 come from Simon Goulart,
    Admirable and Memorable Histories (1607).

 25 *Paracelsus* Swiss physician and alchemist (1493–1541), famous as a serious sci-
    entist and physician while also the subject of many tall stories.

 31 *what's ... me* There are proverbs, 'to be afraid of one's own shadow' and 'to
    fight with one's own shadow', but closer to the case of Ferdinand is an emblem
    for guilt in Whitney's *Choice of Emblemes* showing a man holding a sword fear-
    ing his own shadow. See R. E. R. Madelaine, *N&Q* 227, 1982, p. 146.

MALATESTE
  Nothing, my lord.
FERDINAND
  Yes.
MALATESTE
  'Tis your shadow.
FERDINAND
  Stay it, let it not haunt me.   35
MALATESTE
  Impossible, if you move, and the sun shine.
FERDINAND
  I will throttle it.
                    [*Throws himself on the ground*]
MALATESTE
  Oh, my lord, you are angry with nothing.
FERDINAND
  You are a fool. How is't possible I should catch my shadow
  unless I fall upon't? When I go to hell, I mean to carry a   40
  bribe, for look you, good gifts evermore make way for the
  worst persons.
PESCARA
  Rise, good my lord.
FERDINAND
  I am studying the art of patience.
PESCARA
  'Tis a noble virtue.   45
FERDINAND
  To drive six snails before me, from this town to Moscow –
  neither use goad nor whip to them, but let them take their
  own time – the patient'st man i'th'world match me for an
  experiment – and I'll crawl after like a sheep-biter.
CARDINAL
  Force him up.   50
                    [*They get* FERDINAND *to his feet*]
FERDINAND
  Use me well, you were best: what I have done, I have done,
  I'll confess nothing.
DOCTOR
  Now let me come to him. Are you mad, my lord? Are you
  out of your princely wits?
FERDINAND
  What's he?   55

---

49 *sheep-biter* dog that bites or worries sheep
51–2 *what ... nothing* Recalling *Othello*, V.ii.303–4.

PESCARA
Your doctor.

FERDINAND
Let me have his beard sawed off, and his eye-brows filed
more civil.

DOCTOR
I must do mad tricks with him, for that's the only way on't.
I have brought your grace a salamander's skin, to keep you   60
from sun-burning.

FERDINAND
I have cruel sore eyes.

DOCTOR
The white of a cocatrice's egg is present remedy.

FERDINAND
Let it be a new laid one, you were best. – Hide me from
him. Physicians are like kings, they brook no contradiction.   65

DOCTOR
Now he begins to fear me, now let me alone with him.

CARDINAL
How now, put off your gown?

DOCTOR
Let me have some forty urinals filled with rose water: he
and I'll go pelt one another with them. Now he begins to
fear me. – Can you fetch a frisk, sir? – Let him go, let him   70
go, upon my peril.

                    [*They release* FERDINAND]
I find by his eye he stands in awe of me, I'll make him as
tame as a dormouse.

                    [FERDINAND *attacks the* DOCTOR]

FERDINAND
Can you fetch your frisks, sir? I will stamp him into a cullis,
flay off his skin to cover one of the anatomies this rogue   75
hath set i'th'cold yonder – in Barber Surgeons' hall! Hence!

---

57 NCW suggest that if the part of Doctor is doubled by the boy-actor who earlier
     played Cariola, the exaggerated false beard and eyebrows (conventional comedy
     make-up) make appropriate heavy disguise for the actor.

60 *salamander's* The salamander was believed to live in fire.

63 *Cockatrice's* The basilisk's – see III.ii.87n.

70 *fetch a frisk* cut a caper – dance a jigury

74 *cullis* meat broth

75 *anatomies* skeletons

76 *Barber Surgeons' hall* This chartered company was entitled to claim four corpses
     of executed felons per year for surgical dissection and experiment: it displayed
     specimen skeletons in the company's hall in Monkswell Street, Cripplegate.

Hence! You are all of you like beasts for sacrifice! There's
nothing left of you but tongue and belly, flattery and
lechery!   [*Exit*]

PESCARA
Doctor, he did not fear you throughly.   80

DOCTOR
True, I was somewhat too forward.   [*Exit*]

BOSOLA
[*Aside*] Mercy upon me, what a fatal judgement
Hath fallen upon this Ferdinand.

PESCARA   Knows your grace
What accident hath brought unto the Prince
This strange distraction?   85

CARDINAL
[*Aside*] I must feign somewhat. [*Aloud*] Thus they say it
     grew:
You have heard it rumoured for these many years,
None of our family dies but there is seen
The shape of an old woman, which is given
By tradition to us, to have been murdered   90
By her nephews for her riches. Such a figure
One night, as the Prince sat up late at's book,
Appeared to him: when crying out for help,
The gentlemen of's chamber found his grace
All on a cold sweat, altered much in face   95
And language; since which apparition
He hath grown worse and worse, and I much fear
He cannot live.

BOSOLA
[*To* CARDINAL] Sir, I would speak with you.

PESCARA   We'll leave your
     grace,
Wishing to the sick Prince, our noble lord,   100
All health of mind and body.

CARDINAL   You are most welcome.

[*Exeunt all except* CARDINAL *and* BOSOLA]

Are you come? [Aside] So: this fellow must not know
By any means I had intelligence
In our Duchess' death, for though I counselled it,
The full of all th'engagement seemed to grow   105
From Ferdinand. [*To* BOSOLA] Now sir, how fares our
     sister?
I do not think but sorrow makes her look

Like to an oft-dyed garment: she shall now
Taste comfort from me. Why do you look so wildly?
Oh, the fortune of your master here, the Prince,   110
Dejects you? But be you of happy comfort.
If you'll do one thing for me, I'll entreat
Though he had a cold tombstone o'er his bones
I'd make you what you would be.

BOSOLA   Any thing:
Give it me in a breath, and let me fly to't.   115
They that think long, small expedition win,
For musing much o'th'end, cannot begin.

[*Enter* JULIA]

JULIA
Sir, will you come in to supper?

CARDINAL   I am busy, leave me.

JULIA
[*Aside*] What an excellent shape hath that fellow!   *Exit*

CARDINAL
'Tis thus: Antonio lurks here in Milan,   120
Enquire him out, and kill him. While he lives
Our sister cannot marry, and I have thought
Of an excellent match for her. Do this, and style me
Thy advancement.

BOSOLA   But by what means shall I find him out?

CARDINAL
There is a gentleman called Delio   125
Here in the camp, that hath been long approved
His loyal friend: set eye upon that fellow,
Follow him to Mass; may be Antonio,
Although he do account religion
But a school-name, for fashion of the world,   130
May accompany him; or else go enquire out
Delio's confessor, and see if you can bribe
Him to reveal it. There are a thousand ways
A man might find to trace him, as to know
What fellows haunt the Jews for taking up   135
Great sums of money – for sure he's in want –

---

112 *one* ed. (on Q1)

126 *camp* Reminding the audience that the Cardinal has turned soldier (Brennan).

130 *school-name* From Sidney, *Arcadia* (*Works* II. 133): 'As for vertue, hee counted
     it but a schoole name' – a disparaging reference to the 'Schoolmen' of scholastic
     philosophy. Brown cites Bacon's view that they produced 'cobwebs of learning,
     admirable for the fineness of thread and work, but of no substance or profit'
     (*Advancement of Learning* I).

Or else to go to th'picture makers and learn
Who brought her picture lately – some of these
Happily may take.
BOSOLA   Well, I'll not freeze i'th' business,
  I would see that wretched thing Antonio   140
  Above all sights i'th'world.
CARDINAL   Do, and be happy.   *Exit*
BOSOLA
  This fellow doth breed basilisks in's eyes,
  He's nothing else but murder; yet he seems
  Not to have notice of the Duchess' death.
  'Tis his cunning: I must follow his example,   145
  There cannot be a surer way to trace
  Than that of an old fox.

              [*Enter* JULIA *pointing a pistol at him*]

JULIA   So, sir, you are well met.
BOSOLA
  How now?
JULIA   Nay, the doors are fast enough.
  Now sir, I will make you confess your treachery.
BOSOLA
  Treachery?
JULIA   Yes, confess to me   150
  Which of my women 'twas you hired, to put
  Love-powder into my drink?
BOSOLA   Love powder?
JULIA
  Yes, when I was at Malfi,
  Why should I fall in love with such a face else?
  I have already suffered for thee so much pain,   155
  The only remedy to do me good
  Is to kill my longing.
BOSOLA   Sure your pistol holds
  Nothing but perfumes or kissing comfits; excellent lady,
  You have a pretty way on't to discover
  Your longing: come, come, I'll disarm you,   160
  And arm you thus. [*Embracing her*] Yet this is wondrous
    strange.

---

142 *basilisks* See III.ii.87n.
147 s.d. Webster's stagecraft makes Julia's return parallel with Antonio's return, also
     carrying a pistol, in III.ii.140. Then Julia's wooing of Bosola is parallel (though
     clearly contrasting) to that of the Duchess' wooing of Antonio in Act I.
158 *kissing comfits* sweets perfumed to sweeten the breath

JULIA

    Compare thy form and my eyes together,
    You'll find my love no such great miracle. Now you'll say
    I am wanton; this nice modesty in ladies
    Is but a troublesome familiar   165
    That haunts them.

BOSOLA

    Know you me. I am a blunt soldier.

JULIA   The better,

    Sure. There wants fire, where there are no lively sparks
    Of roughness.

BOSOLA   And I want compliment.

JULIA

    Why, ignorance in courtship cannot make you do amiss   170
    If you have a heart to do well.

BOSOLA   You are very fair.

JULIA

    Nay, if you lay beauty to my charge
    I must plead unguilty.

BOSOLA   Your bright eyes

    Carry a quiver of darts in them sharper
    Than sun-beams.

JULIA   You will mar me with commendation,   175

    Put yourself to the charge of courting me,
    Whereas now I woo you.

BOSOLA

    [*Aside*] I have it, I will work upon this creature. –
    [*To* JULIA] Let us grow most amorously familiar.
    If the great Cardinal now should see me thus,   180
    Would he not count me a villain?

JULIA

    No, he might count me a wanton,
    Not lay a scruple of offence on you:
    For if I see and steal a diamond,
    The fault is not i'th'stone but in me the thief   185
    That purloins it. I am sudden with you:
    We that are great women of pleasure, use to cut off
    These uncertain wishes and unquiet longings
    And in an instant join the sweet delight
    And the pretty excuse together. Had you been in th'street,   190
    Under my chamber window, even there
    I should have courted you.

168–9 *fire ... roughness* From Sidney, *Arcadia* (*Works* I. 452–3).
170–1 *ignorance ... well* From Sidney, *Arcadia* (*Works* I. 106).
188–90 *wishes ... excuse* From Sidney, *Arcadia* (*Works* I. 452).

BOSOLA   Oh, you are an excellent lady.
JULIA
　Bid me do somewhat for you presently
　To express I love you.
BOSOLA   I will; and if you love me,
　Fail not to effect it.   195
　The Cardinal is grown wondrous melancholy:
　Demand the cause, let him not put you off
　With feigned excuse; discover the main ground on't.
JULIA
　Why would you know this?
BOSOLA   I have depended on him,
　And I hear that he is fallen in some disgrace   200
　With the Emperor. If he be, like the mice
　That forsake falling houses, I would shift
　To other dependence.
JULIA   You shall not need follow the wars,
　I'll be your maintenance.
BOSOLA   And I your loyal servant;
　But I cannot leave my calling.
JULIA   Not leave an   205
　Ungrateful general, for the love of a sweet lady?
　You are like some cannot sleep in feather-beds,
　But must have blocks for their pillows.
BOSOLA   Will you do this?
JULIA
　Cunningly.
BOSOLA   Tomorrow I'll expect th'intelligence.
JULIA
　Tomorrow? Get you into my cabinet,   210
　You shall have it with you. Do not delay me,
　No more than I do you. I am like one
　That is condemned: I have my pardon promised,
　But I would see it sealed. Go, get you in,
　You shall see me wind my tongue about his heart   215
　Like a skein of silk.

                                        [*Exit* BOSOLA]

            [*Enter* CARDINAL *followed by* SERVANTS]

CARDINAL
　Where are you?
SERVANTS   Here.

195–6 ed. (one line Q1)
211–14 *delay … sealed* From Sidney, *Arcadia* (*Works* II. 31).

CARDINAL   Let none upon your lives
  Have conference with the Prince Ferdinand
  Unless I know it.

                              [*Exeunt* SERVANTS]

        [*Aside*] In this distraction
  He may reveal the murder.   220
  Yond's my lingering consumption:
  I am weary of her and by any means
  Would be quit off.
JULIA   How now, my lord,
  What ails you?
CARDINAL   Nothing.
JULIA   Oh, you are much altered.
  Come, I must be your secretary and remove   225
  This lead from off your bosom. What's the matter?
CARDINAL
  I may not tell you.
JULIA   Are you so far in love with sorrow
  You cannot part with part of it? Or think you
  I cannot love your grace when you are sad,
  As well as merry? Or do you suspect   230
  I, that have been a secret to your heart
  These many winters, cannot be the same
  Unto your tongue?
CARDINAL   Satisfy thy longing,
  The only way to make thee keep my counsel
  Is not to tell thee.
JULIA   Tell your echo this –   235
  Or flatterers, that like echoes still report
  What they hear, though most imperfect – and not me:
  For if that you be true unto yourself,
  I'll know.
CARDINAL Will you rack me?
JULIA   No, judgement shall
  Draw it from you. It is an equal fault,   240
  To tell one's secrets unto all, or none.
CARDINAL
  The first argues folly.
JULIA   But the last tyranny.
CARDINAL
  Very well – why, imagine I have committed
  Some secret deed which I desire the world
  May never hear of.
JULIA   Therefore may not I know it?   245
  You have concealed for me as great a sin

As adultery: sir, never was occasion
For perfect trial of my constancy
Till now: sir, I beseech you.
CARDINAL   You'll repent it.
JULIA   Never.
CARDINAL
It hurries thee to ruin. I'll not tell thee,   250
Be well advised, and think what danger 'tis
To receive a prince's secrets: they that do
Had need have their breasts hooped with adamant
To contain them. I pray thee yet be satisfied,
Examine thine own frailty; 'tis more easy   255
To tie knots than unloose them: 'tis a secret
That like a ling'ring poison may chance lie
Spread in thy veins, and kill thee seven year hence.
JULIA
Now you dally with me.
CARDINAL   No more: thou shalt know it.
By my appointment the great Duchess of Malfi   260
And two of her young children, four nights since
Were strangled.
JULIA   Oh heaven! Sir, what have you done!
CARDINAL
How now, how settles this? Think you, your
Bosom will be a grave dark and obscure enough
For such a secret?
JULIA   You have undone yourself, sir.   265
CARDINAL
Why?
JULIA   It lies not in me to conceal it.
CARDINAL
No? Come, I will swear you to't upon this book.
JULIA
Most religiously.
CARDINAL   Kiss it.

[She kisses the book]

Now you shall never utter it. Thy curiosity
Hath undone thee. Thou'rt poisoned with that book;   270
Because I knew thou couldst not keep my counsel,
I have bound thee to't by death.

---

268 *religiously* If Julia kneels the spectators will recognise a visual parallel with the
    death of the Duchess; at the same time Julia dies with the conventional words of
    a dying sinner, contrasting to the firm faith of the Duchess.
272 *thee* ed. (the Q1)

[*Enter* BOSOLA]

BOSOLA
  For pity sake, hold!
CARDINAL   Ha, Bosola!
JULIA   I forgive you
  This equal piece of justice you have done,
  For I betrayed your counsel to that fellow,   275
  He overheard it: that was the cause I said
  It lay not in me to conceal it.
BOSOLA   Oh foolish woman,
  Couldst not thou have poisoned him?
JULIA   'Tis weakness
  Too much to think what should have been done.
  I go I know not whither.   [*She dies*] 280
CARDINAL
  Wherefore com'st thou hither?
BOSOLA
  That I might find a great man like yourself,
  Not out of his wits as the Lord Ferdinand,
  To remember my service.
CARDINAL   I'll have thee hewed in pieces!
BOSOLA
  Make not yourself such a promise of that life   285
  Which is not yours to dispose of.
CARDINAL
  Who placed thee here?
BOSOLA   Her lust, as she intended.
CARDINAL
  Very well, now you know me for your fellow murderer.
BOSOLA
  And wherefore should you lay fair marble colours
  Upon your rotten purposes to me,   290
  Unless you imitate some that do plot great treasons
  And, when they have done, go hide themselves i'th'graves
  Of those were actors in't?
CARDINAL   No more,
  There is a fortune attends thee.
BOSOLA
  Shall I go sue to Fortune any longer?   295
  'Tis the fool's pilgrimage.
CARDINAL
  I have honours in store for thee.

289–90 A further metaphor from painting, the wording close to Sidney, *Arcadia*,
  (*Works* I. 260).

BOSOLA

There are a many ways that conduct to seeming
Honour, and some of them very dirty ones.

CARDINAL

Throw to the devil   300
Thy melancholy. The fire burns well,
What need we keep a stirring of it, and make
A greater smother? Thou wilt kill Antonio?

BOSOLA

Yes.

CARDINAL Take up that body.

BOSOLA   I think I shall
Shortly grow the common bier for church-yards.   305

CARDINAL

I will allow thee some dozen of attendants
To aid thee in the murder.

BOSOLA   Oh, by no means.
Physicians that apply horse-leeches to any rank swelling,
use to cut off their tails, that the blood may run through
them the faster: let me have no train when I go to shed 310
blood, lest it make me have a greater when I ride to the
gallows.

CARDINAL

Come to me after midnight to help remove that body to her
own lodging: I'll give out she died o'th'plague, 'twill breed
the less enquiry after her death.   315

BOSOLA

Where's Castruchio, her husband?

CARDINAL

He's rode to Naples to take possession of Antonio's citadel.

BOSOLA

Believe me, you have done a very happy turn.

CARDINAL

Fail not to come. There is the master-key
Of our lodgings, and by that you may conceive   320
What trust I plant in you.   *Exit*

BOSOLA   You shall find me ready.
Oh poor Antonio, though nothing be so needful
To thy estate as pity, yet I find
Nothing so dangerous. I must look to my footing;

298–9 For the proverbial quality of this remark compare Francis Bacon's observation
   that the ways to enrich are many and most of them foul.

308–17 ed. (as verse Q1)

319 *master key* A parallel to Bosola's procuring for Ferdinand the key to the
   Duchess' bedchamber in III.i.80.

In such slippery ice-pavements men had need   325
To be frost-nailed well, they may break their necks else.
The precedent's here afore me: how this man
Bears up in blood, seems fearless! Why, 'tis well:
Security some men call the suburbs of hell,
Only a dead wall between. Well, good Antonio,   330
I'll seek thee out, and all my care shall be
To put thee into safety from the reach
Of these most cruel biters that have got
Some of thy blood already. It may be
I'll join with thee in a most just revenge: 335
The weakest arm is strong enough that strikes
With the sword of justice. – Still methinks the Duchess
Haunts me! There there, 'tis nothing but my melancholy.
O penitence, let me truly taste thy cup,
That throws men down, only to raise them up.   340

Exit [with JULIA's *body]*

[Act V,] Scene iii

[Enter ANTONIO *and* DELIO]

DELIO
Yond's the Cardinal's window. This fortification

327 *precedent's* ed. (President's Q1)
328 *Bears ... blood* Probably deriving from hunting terms – 'keeps his courage' (so
    Lucas); Brown suggests 'persists in shedding blood'.
329 *Security* If of the spiritual kind, security was believed dangerous because imply-
    ing undue confidence in salvation; if carnal, dangerous because implying undue
    concern for this life and indifference to the next world.
330 *dead* continuous
340 s.d. A visual parallel to Bosola's previous exit with the Duchess' body in IV.ii.

  0 s.d. ed. (SCENA III. / *Antonio, Delio, Eccho, (from the Dutchesse Graue.)* Q1).
    The s.d. in Q seems to be directed to readers; it makes no reference to any visual
    special effect, and Delio does say (45) that Antonio only imagines seeing the
    Duchess' face; but Antonio's description (43–4), as Brown notes, corresponds to
    a s.d. in *The Second Maiden's Tragedy* (acted by the King's Men in 1611): *On a
    sodayne in a kinde of Noyse like a Wynde, the dores clattering, the Toombstone
    flies open, and a great light appeares in the midst of the Toombe; His Lady as
    went owt, standing iust before hym all in white, Stuck with Iewells and a great
    crucifex on her brest.* Webster perhaps saw this piece of machinery among the
    properties of the King's Men.
  1 *Yond* In the original performance Delio presumably would point to the tiring-

Grew from the ruins of an ancient abbey,
And to yond side o'th'river lies a wall,
Piece of a cloister, which in my opinion
Gives the best echo that you ever heard,   5
So hollow and so dismal and withal
So plain in the distinction of our words
That many have supposed it is a spirit
That answers.

ANTONIO   I do love these ancient ruins.
We never tread upon them but we set   10
Our foot upon some reverend history,
And questionless, here in this open court
Which now lies naked to the injuries
Of stormy weather, some men lie interred
Loved the church so well, and gave so largely to't,   15
They thought it should have canopied their bones
Till doomsday; but all things have their end:
Churches and cities, which have diseases like to men,
Must have like death that we have.

ECHO   *Like death that we have.*

DELIO
Now the echo hath caught you.

ANTONIO   It groaned, methought, and
          gave   20
A very deadly accent.

ECHO   *Deadly accent.*

DELIO
I told you 'twas a pretty one: you may make it
A huntsman, or a falconer, a musician,
Or a thing of sorrow.

ECHO   *A thing of sorrow.*

ANTONIO
Ay sure, that suits it best.

ECHO   *That suits it best.*   25

ANTONIO
'Tis very like my wife's voice.

---

house backing the stage (with its openings at the upper level) to indicate the
exterior of the Cardinal's house. Antonio's reference to *here in this open court*
presumably indicates the main stage where they stand; other features – the wall
and *piece of a cloister* – could be left wholly to the spectator's imagination. The
echoes would be spoken off-stage by the actor who played the Duchess. If an
actual tomb-property was used, it was probably placed in the central opening in
the tiring-house.

9–11 From Montaigne, *Essayes*, III.ix, p. 596–7.

ECHO   *Ay, wife's voice.*
DELIO
 Come: let's walk farther from't.
 I would not have you go to th'Cardinal's tonight:
 Do not.
ECHO *Do not.*
DELIO
 Wisdom doth not more moderate wasting sorrow   30
 Than time: take time for't, be mindful of thy safety.
ECHO
Be mindful of thy safety.
ANTONIO   Necessity compels me.
 Make scrutiny throughout the passes
 Of your own life; you'll find it impossible
 To fly your fate.
[ECHO]   *O fly your fate.*   35
DELIO
 Hark: the dead stones seem to have pity on you
 And give you good counsel.
ANTONIO   Echo, I will not talk with thee,
 For thou art a dead thing.
ECHO   *Thou art a dead thing.*
ANTONIO
 My Duchess is asleep now,
 And her little ones, I hope sweetly: oh heaven   40
 Shall I never see her more?
ECHO   *Never see her more.*
ANTONIO
 I marked not one repetition of the echo
 But that: and on the sudden a clear light
 Presented me a face folded in sorrow.
DELIO
 Your fancy, merely.
ANTONIO   Come, I'll be out of this ague;   45
 For to live thus is not indeed to live:
 It is a mockery and abuse of life.
 I will not henceforth save myself by halves,
 Lose all, or nothing.

27 *let's* ed. (let's us Q1)
28 *go* Q1b (too Q1a)
33 *passes* events
35 s.p. ed. (not in Q1)
41 *never see her more* Antonio echoes his own words at III.v.82.
43–4 See n. to O s.d. above.

DELIO   Your own virtue save you!
  I'll fetch your eldest son and second you: 50
  It may be that the sight of his own blood
  Spread in so sweet a figure, may beget
  The more compassion.
[ANTONIO]   How ever, fare you well.
  Though in our miseries Fortune have a part,
  Yet in our noble suff'rings she hath none.   55
  Contempt of pain – that we may call our own.

Exeunt

[Act V,] Scene iv

[*Enter* CARDINAL, PESCARA, MALATESTE, RODERIGO,
and GRISOLAN]

CARDINAL
  You shall not watch tonight by the sick Prince,
  His grace is very well recovered.
MALATESTE
  Good my lord, suffer us.
CARDINAL   Oh, by no means.
  The noise, and change of object in his eye,
  Doth more distract him. I pray, all to bed,   5
  And though you hear him in his violent fit,
  Do not rise, I entreat you.
PESCARA   So sir, we shall not.
CARDINAL
  Nay, I must have your promise
  Upon your honours, for I was enjoined to't
  By himself; and he seemed to urge it sensibly.   10
PESCARA
  Let our honours bind this trifle.

---

53 s.p. ed. (not in Q1)

  0 s.d. ed. (SCENA. IIII. / *Cardinall, Pescara, Malateste, Roderigo, Grisolan, Bosola, Ferdinand, Antonio, Seruant.* Q1)
  1 *tonight* The time is close to midnight (see line 23). Since performances at the open amphitheatre playhouses took place in daylight, and the Blackfriars theatre auditorium was candle-lit not darkened, actors carried torches, candles or (as here) lanterns, as conventional indication of night.
  10 *sensibly* with strong feeling
  11 *our* ed. (out Q1)

CARDINAL
  Nor any of your followers.
MALATESTE   Neither.
CARDINAL
  It may be, to make trial of your promise
  When he's asleep, myself will rise and feign
  Some of his mad tricks, and cry out for help,   15
  And feign myself in danger.
MALATESTE   If your throat were cutting
  I'd not come at you, now I have protested against it.
CARDINAL
  Why, I thank you.   [*Walks apart*]
GRISOLAN   'Twas a foul storm tonight.
RODERIGO
  The Lord Ferdinand's chamber shook like an osier.
MALATESTE
  'Twas nothing but pure kindness in the devil,   20
  To rock his own child.

                          Exeunt [all but CARDINAL]

CARDINAL
  The reason why I would not suffer these
  About my brother, is, because at midnight
  I may with better privacy convey
  Julia's body to her own lodging.   25
  Oh, my conscience!
  I would pray now, but the devil takes away my heart
  For having any confidence in prayer.

                    [*Enter* BOSOLA *behind*]

  About this hour I appointed Bosola
  To fetch the body: when he hath served my turn,   30
  He dies.   *Exit*
BOSOLA
  Ha? 'Twas the Cardinal's voice: I heard him name
  Bosola, and my death. – Listen, I hear one's footing.

                    [*Enter* FERDINAND]

FERDINAND
  Strangling is a very quiet death.
BOSOLA
  [*Aside*] Nay then, I see I must stand upon my guard.   35

---

16 *cutting* being cut
25–6 ed. (one line Q1)
34 *quiet* ed. (quiein Q1)

FERDINAND
    What say to that? Whisper, softly: do you agree to't?
    So. It must be done i'th'dark – the Cardinal
    Would not for a thousand pounds the Doctor should see it.
                                                        Exit

BOSOLA
    My death is plotted. Here's the consequence of murder.
    'We value not desert, nor Christian breath,   40
    When we know black deeds must be cured with death'.

                [*Enter* ANTONIO *and* SERVANT]

SERVANT
    Here stay sir, and be confident, I pray.
    I'll fetch you a dark lantern.   *Exit*
ANTONIO
    Could I take him at his prayers,
    There were hope of pardon.
BOSOLA   Fall right my sword: 45
    I'll not give thee so much leisure as to pray.

                [BOSOLA *wounds* ANTONIO]

ANTONIO
    Oh, I am gone! Thou hast ended a long suit
    In a minute.
BOSOLA   What art thou?
ANTONIO   A most wretched thing,
    That only have thy benefit in death,
    To appear myself.

                [*Enter* SERVANT *with a lantern*]

SERVANT   Where are you sir?   50
ANTONIO
    Very near my home. – Bosola?
SERVANT   Oh misfortune!
BOSOLA
    Smother thy pity, thou art dead else. – Antonio?
    The man I would have saved 'bove mine own life?
    We are merely the stars' tennis balls, struck and banded

45–6 Bosola, unable to identify the speaker in the darkness, mistakes Antonio for a
    cut-throat and misinterprets his words as meaning 'If I could kill Bosola at his
    prayers the Cardinal would give me a pardon'.
54–5 A Renaissance tag, but the phrasing is very close to Sidney, *Arcadia* (*Works*
    II. 177), where men 'are but like tenisballs, tossed by the racket of the hyer
    powers'; see also Alexander, *The Alexandraean Tragedy*, 5.1: 'I thinke the world
    is but a tennis-court, / Where men are tossde by fortune as her balls'.

Which way please them. Oh good Antonio,   55
I'll whisper one thing in thy dying ear
Shall make thy heart break quickly: thy fair Duchess
And two sweet children –
ANTONIO   Their very names
Kindle a little life in me –
BOSOLA   Are murdered!
ANTONIO
Some men have wished to die   60
At the hearing of sad tidings. I am glad
That I shall do't in sadness. I would not now
Wish my wounds balmed, nor healed, for I have no use
To put my life to: in all our quest of greatness,
Like wanton boys whose pastime is their care,   65
We follow after bubbles blown in the air.
Pleasure of life, what is't? Only the good hours
Of an ague; merely a preparative to rest,
To endure vexation. I do not ask
The process of my death: only commend me   70
To Delio.
BOSOLA   Break heart.
ANTONIO
And let my son fly the courts of princes.   [Dies]
BOSOLA
Thou seem'st to have loved Antonio?
SERVANT   I brought him hither
To have reconciled him to the Cardinal.
BOSOLA
I do not ask thee that: 75
Take him up, if thou tender thine own life,
And bear him where the Lady Julia
Was wont to lodge. Oh, my fate moves swift.
I have this Cardinal in the forge already,
Now I'll bring him to th'hammer. Oh direful misprision, 80
I will not imitate things glorious
No more than base; I'll be mine own example.
[To SERVANT] On, on, and look thou represent, for silence,
The thing thou bear'st.

Exeunt [BOSOLA *and* SERVANT *with* ANTONIO's *body*]

---

59 A contrast to the comforting words Bosola speaks to the dying Duchess at
    IV.ii.340–43. Delivered abruptly, the line can provoke laughter in an audience.

62 *sadness* earnest

80 *misprision* mistake

84 s.d. Webster's stagecraft makes a point by repetition: Bosola has already carried
    out the dead bodies of the Duchess (IV.ii) and Julia (V.ii).

[Act V,] Scene v

[*Enter* CARDINAL, *with a book*]

CARDINAL
I am puzzled in a question about hell:
He says, in hell there's one material fire,
And yet it shall not burn all men alike.
Lay him by. How tedious is a guilty conscience!
When I look into the fish-ponds in my garden   5
Methinks I see a thing armed with a rake
That seems to strike at me.

[*Enter* BOSOLA *and* SERVANT *with* ANTONIO's *body*]

Now! Art thou come? Thou look'st ghastly:
There sits in thy face some great determination,
Mixed with some fear.
BOSOLA   Thus it lightens into action: 10
I am come to kill thee.
CARDINAL   Ha? Help! Our guard!
BOSOLA
Thou art deceived, they are out of thy howling.
CARDINAL
Hold: and I will faithfully divide
Revenues with thee.
BOSOLA   Thy prayers and proffers
Are both unseasonable.
CARDINAL   Raise the watch!   15
We are betrayed!
BOSOLA   I have confined your flight:
I'll suffer your retreat to Julia's chamber,
But no further.
CARDINAL   Help! We are betrayed!

[*Enter, above,* PESCARA, MALATESTE, RODERIGO,
GRISOLAN]

MALATESTE   Listen.

---

0 s.d. ed. (SCENA. V. / *Cardinall (with a Booke) Bosola, Pescara, Malateste,
Rodorigo, Ferdinand, Delio, Seruant with Antonio's body.* Q1)
with a book a conventional stage sign of melancholy (as in *Hamlet*, 2.2.167)
4 *tedious* If the Cardinal uses the word in the sense 'tiresome' he is being cynical,
if in the sense 'painful', he is seriously troubled. Either is possible.
12 ed. (Thou ... deceiu'd: / They ... howling. Q1)

CARDINAL
  My dukedom, for rescue!
RODERIGO   Fie upon his counterfeiting.
MALATESTE
  Why, 'tis not the Cardinal.
RODERIGO   Yes, yes, 'tis he: 20
  But I'll see him hanged ere I'll go down to him.
CARDINAL
  Here's a plot upon me! I am assaulted! I am lost
  Unless some rescue!
GRISOLAN   He doth this pretty well,
  But it will not serve to laugh me out of mine honour.
CARDINAL
  The sword's at my throat!
RODERIGO   You would not bawl so loud then.   25
MALATESTE
  Come, come, let's go to bed, he told us thus much
      aforehand.
PESCARA
  He wished you should not come at him, but believe't,
  The accent of the voice sounds not in jest.
  I'll down to him, howsoever, and with engines
  Force ope the doors.   [*Exit above*]

RODERIGO   Let's follow him aloof,   30
  And note how the Cardinal will laugh at him.

                                             [*Exeunt above*]

BOSOLA
  There's for you first –

                He kills the SERVANT

  'Cause you shall not unbarricade the door
  To let in rescue.
CARDINAL
  What cause hast thou to pursue my life?
BOSOLA   Look there.   35
CARDINAL
  Antonio?
BOSOLA   Slain by my hand unwittingly.
  Pray, and be sudden. When thou kill'dst thy sister
  Thou took'st from Justice her most equal balance
  And left her nought but her sword.

19 *My . . . rescue* Recalling *Richard III*, V.iv.7.
32–3 ed. (one line Q1)

CARDINAL   Oh mercy!
BOSOLA
  Now it seems thy greatness was only outward,   40
  For thou fall'st faster of thyself than calamity
  Can drive thee. I'll not waste longer time – there!

           [BOSOLA *wounds the* CARDINAL]

CARDINAL
  Thou hast hurt me.
BOSOLA   Again!

           [*Wounds him again*]

CARDINAL   Shall I die like a leveret
  Without any resistance? Help! Help! Help!
  I am slain!

           [*Enter* FERDINAND]

FERDINAND Th'alarum? Give me a fresh horse!   45
  Rally the vaunt-guard, or the day is lost!
  Yield! Yield! I give you the honour of arms,
  Shake my sword over you. Will you yield?
CARDINAL
  Help me! I am your brother.
FERDINAND   The devil?
  My brother fight upon the adverse party?   50
  There flies your ransom!

      He wounds the CARDINAL, *and (in the scuffle) gives*
            BOSOLA *his death wound*

CARDINAL
  Oh justice!
  I suffer now for what hath former been:
  'Sorrow is held the eldest child of sin'.

---

46 Ferdinand (to grotesque and absurd effect) imagines he is on the battlefield (see
   Richard III, V.iii.177, where Richard starts up out of a nightmare crying 'Give
   me another horse!'). For those spectators who recognise the quotation the absur-
   dity will be doubled – Ferdinand believing himself to be a king in a famous
   Shakespeare play and speaking lines from it. In the original production the effect
   would have been further enhanced for those spectators who recognised that the
   actor playing Ferdinand (Burbage), had played the Shakespearean role of
   Richard III.

51 s.d. This scuffle is evidently to be as clumsy and confused as possible, the very
   opposite of high tragic style.

FERDINAND
Now you're brave fellows: Caesar's fortune was harder   55
than Pompey's, Caesar died in the arms of prosperity,
Pompey at the feet of disgrace: you both died in the field.
The pain's nothing: pain, many times, is taken away with
the apprehension of greater – as the tooth-ache with the
sight of a barber that comes to pull it out. There's philos-   60
ophy for you.

BOSOLA
Now my revenge is perfect: sink, thou main cause
Of my undoing!

                      He kills FERDINAND

                  The last part of my life
Hath done me best service.

FERDINAND
Give me some wet hay, I am broken winded.   65
I do account this world but a dog-kennel:
I will vault credit and affect high pleasures
Beyond death.

BOSOLA   He seems to come to himself
Now he's so near the bottom.

FERDINAND
My sister! Oh my sister, there's the cause on't!   70
'Whether we fall by ambition, blood, or lust,
Like diamonds we are cut with our own dust'.   [*Dies*]

CARDINAL
Thou hast thy payment too.

BOSOLA
Yes, I hold my weary soul in my teeth,
'Tis ready to part from me. I do glory   75
That thou, which stood'st like a huge pyramid
Begun upon a large and ample base,
Shalt end in a little point, a kind of nothing.

        [*Enter* PESCARA, MALATESTE, RODERIGO, GRISOLAN]

PESCARA
How now, my lord?
MALATESTE   Oh sad disaster.
RODERIGO   How comes this?

55–61 ed. (as verse Q1)
65 *wet hay* Treatment for broken-winded horses recommended in Gervase
    Markham, *Markham's Maister-peece* (1610), p. 101 (so Lucas).
68–9 ed. (Beyond death. / He ... bottom. Q1)
74 *soul ... teeth* From Montaigne, *Essayes*, II. xxxv, p.430.

BOSOLA
Revenge for the Duchess of Malfi, murdered   80
By th'Aragonian brethren; for Antonio,
Slain by this hand; for lustful Julia,
Poisoned by this man; and lastly, for myself,
That was an actor in the main of all,
Much 'gainst mine own good nature, yet i'th'end   85
Neglected.
PESCARA   How now, my lord?
CARDINAL   Look to my brother.
He gave us these large wounds as we were struggling
Here i'th'rushes. And now, I pray, let me
Be laid by, and never thought of.
PESCARA
How fatally, it seems, he did withstand   90
His own rescue!
MALATESTE   Thou wretched thing of blood,
How came Antonio by his death?
BOSOLA
In a mist: I know not how;
Such a mistake as I have often seen
In a play. Oh I am gone.   95
We are only like dead walls, or vaulted graves,
That ruined, yields no echo. Fare you well.
It may be pain but no harm to me, to die
In so good a quarrel. Oh this gloomy world!
In what a shadow, or deep pit of darkness,   100
Doth womanish and fearful mankind live!
Let worthy minds ne'er stagger in distrust
To suffer death or shame for what is just.
Mine is another voyage.   [*Dies*]
PESCARA
The noble Delio, as I came to th'palace,   105
Told me of Antonio's being here, and showed me
A pretty gentleman, his son and heir.

[*Enter* DELIO *with* ANTONIO'S SON]

MALATESTE
Oh sir, you come too late.

---

82 *this* ed. (his Q1)

88 *rushes* Customarily strewn on the Elizabethan stage.

96 *dead* continuous, unbroken

99–101 From Sidney, *Arcadia* (*Works* II. 177): 'such a shadowe, or rather pit of
    darkenes, the wormish mankinde lives'.

DELIO   I heard so, and
    Was armed for't ere I came. Let us make noble use
    Of this great ruin; and join all our force   110
    To establish this young hopeful gentleman
    In's mother's right. These wretched eminent things
    Leave no more fame behind 'em than should one
    Fall in a frost and leave his print in snow:
    As soon as the sun shines, it ever melts,   115
    Both form, and matter. I have ever thought
    Nature doth nothing so great, for great men,
    As when she's pleased to make them lords of truth:
    'Integrity of life is fame's best friend,
    Which nobly, beyond death, shall crown the end'.   120

                                        Exeunt

                        FINIS

112 *mother's right* See IV.ii.273–5n. There is a reference at III.iii.67–8 to the
    Duchess having had a son by her first marriage: a child who, though a minor, is
    Duke of Malfi. Yet the Duchess never refers to any such son by her first marriage
    nor, of course, do the audience see one, whereas Webster stresses the Duchess'
    exceptional concern for her children born of the the marriage to Antonio, and
    their presence in several scenes of the play is very significant. Delio here presents
    Antonio's son, as sole survivor, in public as a symbol of political hope, as suc-
    cessor to his mother. His horoscope – see II.iii.58–66 – may give cause for anx-
    iety, but Webster's treatment of it in Act II is ambivalent. Given the importance
    of this final theatrical and narrative emphasis on the surviving son it seems likely
    that Webster changed his mind during composition of the play and decided to
    diverge from his sources by making the Duchess childless until she married
    Antonio, but he failed to correct the text accordingly. Otherwise the *mother's
    right* would refer, lamely, not to the dukedom, since this has already passed to
    her son by her first marriage (she has only been administering it during his min-
    ority); it would refer only to such property as the Duchess retained personally
    after her marriages. This boy would then represent the (fragile) survival of his
    parents' spiritual values and their love.
117–18 From Sidney, *Arcadia* (*Works* I, p. 190).
119–20 Alluding to Horace, *Odes* I xxii, with a possible ironic implication: see
    Introduction p. xxxiii and Gurr, *Playgoing*, pp. 83–4. Horace's phrase *integer
    vitae* itself was a commonplace, so that probably the implied irony would be
    appreciated only by the more understanding among Webster's audience.